e.explore

Earth

London, New York, Melbourne,
Munich, and Delhi

Project Editor Nigel Ritchie
Editor Richard Williams
Weblink Editors Clare Lister, Mariza O'Keeffe,
Steve Barker, John Bennett

Managing Editor Linda Esposito

Digital Development Manager Fergus Day
DTP Co-ordinator Tony Cutting
DTP Designer Pete Quinlan

Consultant Travis Hudson, Director of Environmental Affairs,
AGI (American Geological Institute)

Category Publisher Sue Grabham

Project Art Editors Jim Green, Jacqui Swan, Joanna Pocock
Senior Designers Smiljka Surla, Yumiko Tahata
Illustrators Mark Longworth, Andrew Kerr, Robin Hunter
Cartography Simon Mumford

Managing Art Editor Sophia M Tampakopoulos Turner

Picture Research Alison Prior
Picture Librarians Sarah Mills, Rose Horridge,
Karl Stange, Kate Ledwith

Production Erica Rosen
Jacket Neal Cobourne

Art Director Simon Webb

First published in Great Britain in 2004 by Dorling Kindersley Limited,
80 Strand, London WC2R 0RL
Penguin Group

Google™ is a trademark of Google Technology Inc.

04 05 06 07 08 09 10 9 8 7 6 5 4 3 2 1

A CIP catalogue for this book is available from the British Library.

ISBN-13: 978-1-40531-545-6
ISBN-10: 1-4053-1545-8

Colour reproduction by Media Development and Printing, UK
Printed in China by Toppan Printing Co. (Shenzen) Ltd.

See our complete catalogue at
www.dk.com

e.explore

Earth

Written by **Matt Turner**

Google

CONTENTS

How to use the e.explore website

e.explore Earth has its own website, created by DK and Google™. When you look up a subject in the book, the article gives you key facts and displays a keyword that links you to extra information online. Just follow these easy steps.

http://www.earth.dke-explore.com

1 Enter this website address...

Address : @ http://www.earth.dke-explore.com

2 Find the keyword in the book...

caves

3 Enter the keyword...

caves

You can use only the keywords from the book to search on our website for the specially selected DK/Google links.

Be safe while you are online:

- Always get permission from an adult before connecting to the internet.

- Never give out personal information about yourself.

- Never arrange to meet someone you have talked to online.

- If a site asks you to log in with your name or email address, ask permission from an adult first.

- Do not reply to emails from strangers – tell an adult.

Parents: Dorling Kindersley actively and regularly reviews and updates the links. However, content may change. Dorling Kindersley is not responsible for any site but its own. We recommend that children are supervised while online, that they do not use Chat Rooms, and that filtering software is used to block unsuitable material.

4   Click on your chosen link...

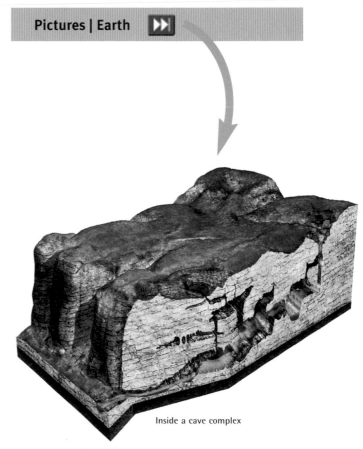

Inside a cave complex

▶▶ Take a virtual tour of a cave

Links include animations, videos, sound buttons, virtual tours, interactive quizzes, databases, timelines, and realtime reports.

5   Download fantastic pictures...

Pictures | Earth ▶▶

The pictures are free of charge, but can be used for personal non-commercial use only.

Go back to the book for your next subject...

EARTH IN THE UNIVERSE

The Universe is everything that exists – all that we see and touch, all energy, all the stars and planets, and all space. It is enormous, stretching into space for at least 15 billion light years in every direction. (One light year is the distance light travels in a year – 9.5 trillion km or 5.9 trillion miles.) The Universe contains countless stars that are clustered in trillions of vast star cities called galaxies. One galaxy is home to our own star – the Sun – and its planets, including Earth.

Universe

BIG BANG ▶
All the galaxies are moving away from one another. This suggests that the Universe was created by an explosion – the Big Bang. In a split-second, the Universe expanded from a speck to a huge fireball of burning gas. Eventually, stars began forming. The Big Bang was 10–20 billion years ago, and most scientists think the Universe will expand forever.

GALAXIES

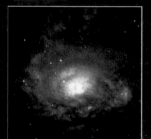

ACTIVE GALAXY
All galaxies give off energy. Some, known as active galaxies, give off very large amounts of energy. The energy may take many different forms, including light and radio waves. The energy pours out from an active galaxy's nucleus, which is thought to contain massive objects.

ANDROMEDA
Andromeda is the nearest galaxy to our own galaxy, called the Milky Way. They belong to the same cluster of galaxies, known as the Local Group. Andromeda is about 2 million light years away from Earth. It is a spiral galaxy and contains hundreds of billions of stars.

TRIANGULUM
The Local Group also contains this spiral galaxy, known as Triangulum. It is about a quarter of the size of the Milky Way. Triangulum is believed to be orbiting (moving around) its neighbour Andromeda, which holds the smaller galaxy in the pull of its gravity.

◀ MILKY WAY
The Milky Way is a galaxy of 200 million stars, including our Sun. It is about 100,000 light years wide. It is a spiral galaxy: a thin disc in which dust and stars form arms revolving around a nucleus (centre). The Sun lies part-way along one arm, which we can see as a pale streak across the night sky. About 70 per cent of all known galaxies are spirals, but some are oval and others are irregular in shape.

AGE OF UNIVERSE (IN BILLIONS OF YEARS)

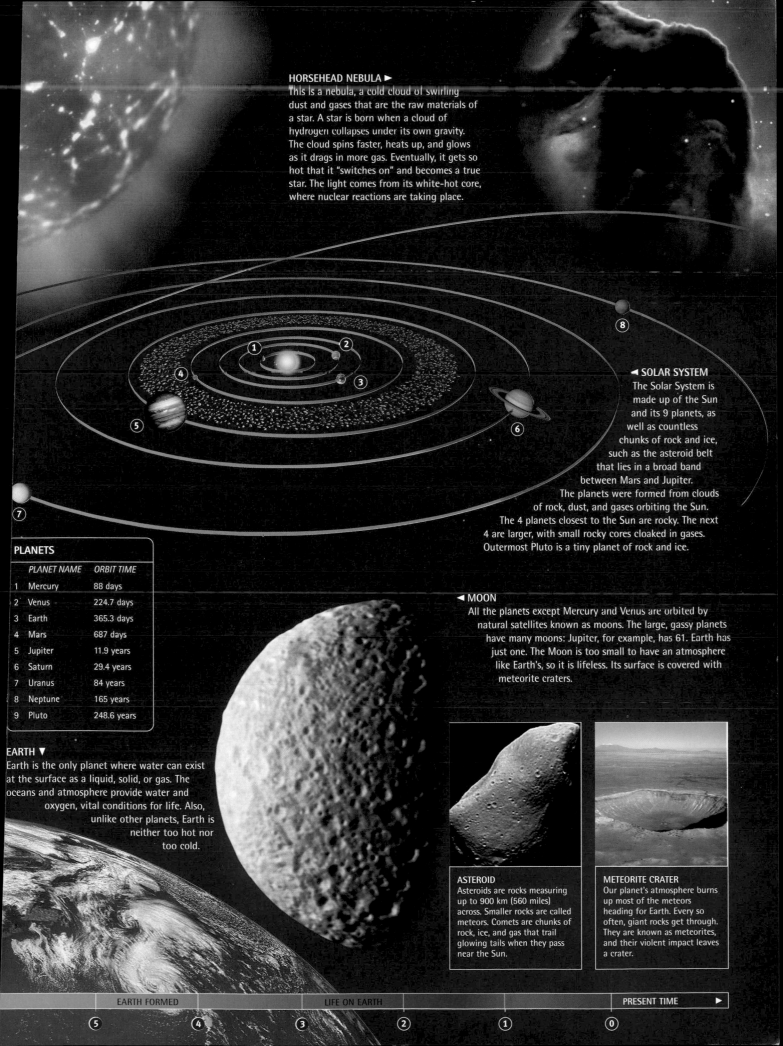

HORSEHEAD NEBULA ▶
This is a nebula, a cold cloud of swirling dust and gases that are the raw materials of a star. A star is born when a cloud of hydrogen collapses under its own gravity. The cloud spins faster, heats up, and glows as it drags in more gas. Eventually, it gets so hot that it "switches on" and becomes a true star. The light comes from its white-hot core, where nuclear reactions are taking place.

◀ SOLAR SYSTEM
The Solar System is made up of the Sun and its 9 planets, as well as countless chunks of rock and ice, such as the asteroid belt that lies in a broad band between Mars and Jupiter. The planets were formed from clouds of rock, dust, and gases orbiting the Sun. The 4 planets closest to the Sun are rocky. The next 4 are larger, with small rocky cores cloaked in gases. Outermost Pluto is a tiny planet of rock and ice.

PLANETS

	PLANET NAME	ORBIT TIME
1	Mercury	88 days
2	Venus	224.7 days
3	Earth	365.3 days
4	Mars	687 days
5	Jupiter	11.9 years
6	Saturn	29.4 years
7	Uranus	84 years
8	Neptune	165 years
9	Pluto	248.6 years

◀ MOON
All the planets except Mercury and Venus are orbited by natural satellites known as moons. The large, gassy planets have many moons: Jupiter, for example, has 61. Earth has just one. The Moon is too small to have an atmosphere like Earth's, so it is lifeless. Its surface is covered with meteorite craters.

EARTH ▼
Earth is the only planet where water can exist at the surface as a liquid, solid, or gas. The oceans and atmosphere provide water and oxygen, vital conditions for life. Also, unlike other planets, Earth is neither too hot nor too cold.

ASTEROID
Asteroids are rocks measuring up to 900 km (560 miles) across. Smaller rocks are called meteors. Comets are chunks of rock, ice, and gas that trail glowing tails when they pass near the Sun.

METEORITE CRATER
Our planet's atmosphere burns up most of the meteors heading for Earth. Every so often, giant rocks get through. They are known as meteorites, and their violent impact leaves a crater.

EARTH FORMED	LIFE ON EARTH		PRESENT TIME ▶
⑤ ④	③ ②	①	⓪

THE SUN AND MOON

Earth is constantly moving around the Sun, completing an orbit (circuit) every year. At the same time, it rotates on its own axis, rather like a spinning top. Together, planet Earth's motions control how its surface is exposed to the Sun's heat and light. They govern the daily rhythm of day and night, the length of each year, and the seasons. The motions are so regular that we set our clocks and live our lives by them. Meanwhile, Earth has its own orbiting body, the Moon, which completes a circuit every month. The pull of its gravity is strong enough to create Earth's ocean tides.

Southern autumnal and northern vernal (spring) equinox

Earth's axis

North Pole

Northern summer, southern winter (North Pole tilts towards Sun)

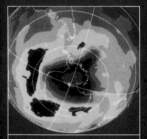

HOLE IN THE OZONE LAYER
Ozone, a form of oxygen found in Earth's atmosphere, protects our health by absorbing harmful radiation. In the 1970s, scientists reported that industrial chemicals known as CFCs were thinning the ozone. In 1985, a hole in the ozone layer was detected over Antarctica. Use of CFCs is now banned.

DAY AND NIGHT ▶
Every 24 hours, Earth makes one rotation about an imaginary line called its axis – a straight line through the poles. This brings daylight to the regions facing the Sun and night to those facing away. Earth rotates in an easterly direction, which means that the Sun always rises over the eastern horizon. Earth's axis is not at right angles to its orbit around the Sun; it is tilted over at an angle of 23.5 degrees from the vertical.

Direction of Earth's spin

RADIATION FROM THE SUN

5% scattered back into space by atmosphere

20% reflected back by clouds

15% absorbed by clouds and atmosphere

5% reflected by surface

5% absorbed by water, dust, and gases in the air

50% absorbed by surface

◀ EARTH'S SEASONS
Earth's axis is tilted towards the Sun, creating different levels of sunlight – which we experience as seasons. When sunlight falls directly on the exposed hemisphere (northern or southern) the day is longer, creating summer conditions. When that pole faces away, sunlight is weaker and the days are shorter, creating winter conditions. At any point in the year, each hemisphere is experiencing opposing seasons.

NORWAY'S MIDNIGHT SUN
The summer Sun is seen at midnight in northern Norway. The far north gets more hours of sunlight than usual during the 6 months in each year when the North Pole is tilted towards the Sun. In high summer, lands in the Arctic Circle enjoy sunlight for 24 hours a day. In midwinter, the Sun does not appear at all.

◀ SOLAR RADIATION
Earth absorbs heat and light from the Sun. Other forms of solar energy reach us too. They include short-wave, high-energy radiation, like gamma rays, x-rays, and ultraviolet (UV) light. This radiation is harmful. For example, UV can give us skin cancers and damage our eyes. The layers of Earth's atmosphere protect us from damage. Earth's upper atmosphere reflects gamma rays and x-rays back into space. Below this, the ozone layer absorbs most of the UV light.

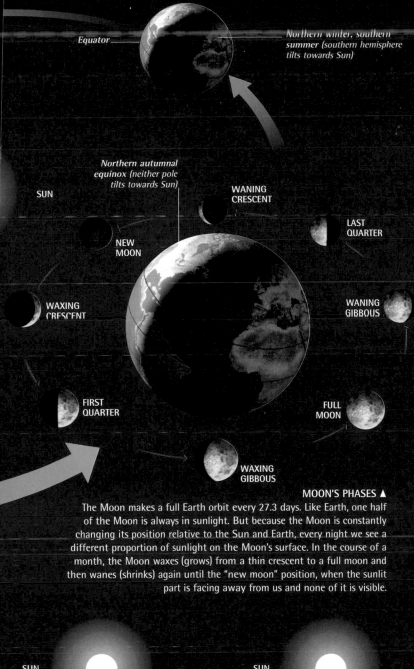

Equator

Northern winter, southern summer (southern hemisphere tilts towards Sun)

Northern autumnal equinox (neither pole tilts towards Sun)

SUN

WANING CRESCENT

LAST QUARTER

NEW MOON

WAXING CRESCENT

WANING GIBBOUS

FIRST QUARTER

FULL MOON

WAXING GIBBOUS

MOON'S PHASES ▲

The Moon makes a full Earth orbit every 27.3 days. Like Earth, one half of the Moon is always in sunlight. But because the Moon is constantly changing its position relative to the Sun and Earth, every night we see a different proportion of sunlight on the Moon's surface. In the course of a month, the Moon waxes (grows) from a thin crescent to a full moon and then wanes (shrinks) again until the "new moon" position, when the sunlit part is facing away from us and none of it is visible.

TEMPERATE SEASONS

SPRING
Temperate lands lying between the tropics (the regions on either side of the equator) and the poles have 4 distinct seasons. In the northern hemisphere, 21 or 22 March is the vernal (spring) equinox: a date when the Sun shines directly on the equator. Now days become longer and warmer, stimulating plant growth.

SUMMER
Summer is the warmest season. In the northern hemisphere, summer occurs between June and September, and in the southern hemisphere, between December and February. On 21 or 22 June, the North Pole is at its maximum tilt towards the Sun. In the northern hemisphere, this is the longest day of the year.

AUTUMN
In autumn, the days grow cooler and longer. The opposite of the vernal equinox is the autumnal equinox, which falls in the northern hemisphere on 22 or 23 September. The shortening hours of daylight lead to a slowdown in plant growth, and many trees shed their leaves in preparation for winter.

WINTER
Winter is the coldest season. On 21 or 22 December (known in the northern hemisphere as the winter solstice), the North Pole is at its maximum tilt away from the Sun. The cold and darkness make some animals hibernate. Others migrate to the southern hemisphere, which is experiencing the warmth of a summer solstice.

SUN

SUN

MOON

Sun and Moon

EARTH

MOON

EARTH

NEAP TIDE (LOWEST)

SPRING TIDE (HIGHEST)

◄ EARTH'S OCEAN TIDES

Every day, Earth's coastlines are washed by the tide – a regular rise and fall in the sea level. As the Moon orbits Earth, the oceans facing it are pulled by lunar gravity, creating a bulge. This brings high tide: a rise in water levels. There is also a matching bulge on the side of Earth facing away from the Moon, caused by the centrifugal force of Earth's rotation. Earth's rotation creates 2 high and 2 low tides every 24 hours. When the Moon and the Sun are in line (twice a month), the combined pull of their gravity creates extra high tides, known as spring tides. Neap tides occur when the gravitational pull of the Moon is weakest.

MAGNETIC EARTH

Magnetism is an invisible force that attracts or repels certain materials, such as iron. The outer part of Earth's hot core is made up mostly of liquid iron. Heat makes the iron swirl about in such a way that it becomes magnetic, turning Earth into a giant magnet. Like any other magnet, Earth has magnetic north and south poles. These lie close to the geographic North and South Poles. Earth's magnetism helps us find our way by using a compass, and it also helps guide some animals when they migrate over long distances.

e ▶▶
magnetic Earth

AURORA ON JUPITER

This intense aurora on Jupiter is caused by solar particles drawn magnetically into the planet's atmosphere. All the planets have magnetic fields. Some are weaker than Earth's; Mars and Venus have weak magnetic fields that may have been stronger when the planets were young. The large planets have much stronger fields. Jupiter's, at 20,000 times greater than Earth's, is the most powerful in the Solar System.

JUPITER

Solar wind: charged particles from the Sun

EARTH'S MAGNETOSPHERE ▶
Earth's magnetic field, known as the magnetosphere (whose boundary is shown in purple), reaches far into space. It protects us from the solar wind: a stream of harmful rays that pours from the Sun. When the rays hit the magnetosphere, they are slowed down and pushed aside, though some are drawn towards the poles. Pressure from the solar wind changes the shape of the magnetosphere, giving it a blunt head and a long tail that streams off into space.

Bow shock helps force the solar wind to go around the magnetosphere

◀ **AURORA AUSTRALIS**
Charged particles from the Sun also affect southern skies, where the lights are known as the aurora australis. At both poles, the light effect often hangs like a vast curtain, but also appears in patches and bands. Auroras are most spectacular when the Sun is particularly active. At these times, massive, violent outbursts of solar energy flood Earth's atmosphere and can cause electrical storms as well.

▲ **AURORA BOREALIS**
This glow in the northern night sky is the aurora borealis, or northern lights. It is caused by electrically charged particles that pour from the Sun at speeds of about 400 km/sec (250 miles/sec). Particles that get close to the polar regions are drawn into the atmosphere by Earth's magnetic field. The disturbed magnetic field flings the particles trapped in it towards Earth, making the upper air glow around the poles.

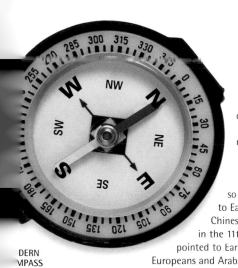

DERN
MPASS

◀ **MAGNETIC NORTH**
A compass is simply a device with a magnetized needle that points to magnetic north, swinging freely on a pivot. The needle lines up with Earth's magnetic field so that its tips always point to Earth's magnetic poles. The Chinese developed the compass in the 11th century. Their compass pointed to Earth's magnetic south pole. Europeans and Arabs preferred their compass to point to Earth's magnetic north pole.

MAGNETITE WITH IRON FILINGS

▲ **MAGNETIC ROCK**
Magnetite, a common source of iron, is a naturally magnetic mineral. It is magnetized by Earth as it lies in the ground. Magnetite is a permanent magnet: it does not lose its magnetism. This is unlike temporary magnets, such as pieces of pure iron, which slowly lose their magnetism after being removed from a forcefield.

COMPASS NAVIGATION
The Ancient Chinese knew about magnetite's unusual qualities in the 4th century BC, but did not develop the compass until the 11th century, when they discovered they could use magnetite to magnetize an iron or steel needle. Europeans and Arabs discovered this independently more than 100 years later.

Incoming solar wind particles create auroras when trapped near the geographic poles

Invisible lines of magnetic force in Earth's magnetic field are drawn into the North Pole and away from the South Pole

Plasma sheet consists of plasma, a form of matter

Magnetotail is where the magnetic field is drawn away by the solar wind

Earth

Solar wind particles deflected by magnetosphere

Van Allen belts (inner and outer) encircle the planet, trapping radiation (energetic, electrically charged particles) in Earth's magnetic field

Lobes with opposing magnetic charges (positive and negative) kept apart by plasma sheet

LOGGERHEAD TURTLE MIGRATION ROUTE

Loggerhead turtles probably use magnetism to find their way in the Atlantic Ocean. After hatching on Florida beaches, baby turtles scuttle towards the waves. Many then spend several years cruising warm currents. A magnetic sense helps them avoid the prevailing northeastern currents heading for Britain, and they continue southwards down the coast of Africa before returning as adults to Florida to breed.

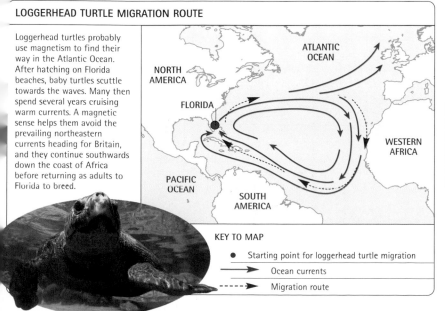

NORTH AMERICA

FLORIDA

ATLANTIC OCEAN

WESTERN AFRICA

PACIFIC OCEAN

SOUTH AMERICA

KEY TO MAP

● Starting point for loggerhead turtle migration

→ Ocean currents

--→ Migration route

▲ **BEACHED WHALE**
Whales regularly become stranded on beaches, either singly or in pods (groups). It has been suggested that they use Earth's magnetic field to navigate while on migration, and this system sometimes lets them down. Though there is no firm proof, research in the 1980s suggested that fin whales may lose their way in areas of weak magnetism. Whales that lose their way may blunder onto a surprise obstacle, such as a low sandbank.

EARTH AND LIFE

Life depends on water in all its forms. Earth is the only planet with water, and the only one known to support life. Earth's temperature is just right for water to be present in the atmosphere, oceans, soil, and icecaps. Covering the planet is a thin layer of life, known as the biosphere. This total life system includes all plants and animals, as well as the non-living materials that form part of the cycle of life.

biosphere

SUN ▶
Water alone is not enough to support life, energy from the Sun is also needed. Plants use sunlight to fuel photosynthesis, the process by which they turn carbon dioxide (CO_2) and water into nutrients. Earth's atmosphere blocks harmful solar energy from reaching the planet, while absorbing sufficient heat and light to nurture life.

BLUE PLANET ▶
From space, Earth is a shimmering blue planet covered in water, and swirling with clouds – evidence of our precious atmosphere. The gases that make up the atmosphere, mostly nitrogen and oxygen, are held in place by gravity. They form a very thin layer, like an envelope around the surface.

Coal formed from carbon

Plants use CO_2

Volcanic eruptions release CO_2 into the atmosphere

CO_2 in rain weathers limestone

Combustion releases CO_2

◀ CARBON CYCLE
Next to water, organic compounds (compounds containing the element carbon) are the most important ingredient of life-forms. Earth's carbon supply is stored in rocks, soil, water, and the atmosphere, as well as in plant and animal tissue. It is readily converted from one form to another, and is recycled constantly through all parts of the biosphere.

→ *Carbon exchange*
→ *Photosynthesis*
→ *Weathering and erosion*
→ *Human carbon transformation*

CO_2 dissolves in water

Carbon from dead matter forms oil and gas

◀ OCEANS
The salty oceans contain about 96.5% of Earth's water. Of the 3.5% that is fresh (non-salty), 1.7% is stored in polar ice, and a similar amount lies in or on the land, such as in rivers and lakes. A tiny amount drifts in the atmosphere. We cannot do without water, as it makes up about 60% by weight of our bodies and plays a role in every biological function.

Plants lose water through transpiration (evaporating from their leaves)

Clouds carry water inland to fall as rain and snow

◀ WATER CYCLE
Water is constantly on the move as a result of solar energy. It evaporates from the oceans, and moves through the atmosphere towards land, where it falls as rain or snow. Some then runs off the surface to form rivers and lakes, which return water to the ocean or the atmosphere. A large amount of rainfall soaks through gaps in the soil to be stored in a vast underground water system.

Rivers and streams return water to seas and oceans

BIOMES

The biosphere is not spread evenly around the planet. Levels of sunlight, temperature, and rainfall differ from one place to another. So, too, do air and ocean currents and land altitudes. The varied conditions create a mosaic of climates, each with its own community of lifeforms. Scientists class the communities in groups called biomes, some of which are shown below.

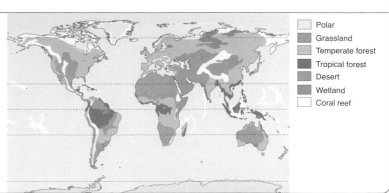

- Polar
- Grassland
- Temperate forest
- Tropical forest
- Desert
- Wetland
- Coral reef

FORESTS ▶

Trees have adapted to survive many climates, from the warm, wet tropics to the cold North. Today, forests cover a quarter of the planet's land area. The richest of all biomes, forests are home to at least 50% of the world's species. They produce nearly half the world's total organic matter and contain about half its total carbon store. Forests prevent soil from being washed away by rain. They also act as Earth's lungs by producing oxygen from carbon dioxide, restoring oxygen levels in the atmosphere.

DESERTS ▶

Deserts include the world's driest lands. They may be hot or cold - even icy - but all are very dry. Nevertheless, life adapts to tough conditions. Plants may grow long roots to reach water deep underground, or lie inactive for years until sudden, brief showers allow them to flower and seed. Desert animals tend to be active at night in order to escape the Sun. Desert ecosystems are very fragile, and overgrazing by livestock may be expanding deserts in sub-Saharan Africa and Central Asia.

GRASSLANDS ▶

Grasslands receive too little rainfall for forest cover, but enough for grasses and shrubs. The plants are adapted to survive poor-quality soil, frequent droughts, and fires. Grasslands include dry grasslands, scrublands, and shrublands. The savannas of sub-Saharan Africa, where grassy plains have a light scattering of trees, are home to rich communities of grazing animals and meat-eaters. Mediterranean-type shrubland grows in climates with cool, wet winters and hot, dry summers.

POLAR REGIONS ▶

The polar regions are the coldest regions on Earth. Antarctica, the southern continent, is cut off from the other landmasses by the stormy Southern Ocean. It is an almost lifeless desert, covered in ice and snow. The Arctic Ocean has a milder climate, especially during the summer, when the tundra teems with life. At both poles, the ocean waters have a high oxygen content, supporting a wide community of animals.

THE AGE OF THE EARTH

Our planet is more than 4.5 billion years old. How do we know this? Geologists study Earth's rocks in order to learn about events that happened in the distant past. They use important changes as markers to divide the planet's long history into several time periods. Placed in a row, the markers make up the geologic timescale.

Geologists use this scale to compare their discoveries and understand the history of Earth.

◄ ARGON DATING
Modern radiometric dating helps to determine the absolute age of rocks. Som elements of rocks are radio active: they break apart an turn into other elements. For instance, potassium-40 breaks down into argon-40 Geologists know how fast i breaks down, so they can d a rock by measuring how much argon-40 it contains.

EARLY LIFE
About 543 million years ago, life on Earth suddenly flourished, as shown by the amazing range of fossils found from that time onward. For the first time, anima had hard body parts, which not only helped them survive but also fossilized well. This picture shows a trilobite: sea-bed scavengers tha teemed in the Cambrian oceans.

FOSSIL ALGAE
The planet's oldest known life-forms are tiny, one-celled organisms such as bacteria and algae. You would need a microscope to study these two-billion-year-old fossil algae found in Precambrian rocks from North America.

e ⏩
Earth's timeline

▲ VOLCANIC BEGINNINGS
At first, the Earth's surface was so hot that it was liquid. As it cooled, the rock hardened. Volcanoes spewed out molten rock and gases: carbon dioxide, nitrogen, and water vapour. Rainfall from the vapour created the oceans. Carbon dioxide dissolved into the oceans, where the first life-forms turned the gas into oxygen.

▲ STROMATOLITES
Stromatolites are mats formed from the dead bodies of algae. The algae live in colonies in shallow water and use sunlight to make energy. Stromatolites are some of the world's oldest fossils, found in rocks up to 3.5 billion years old. Living stromatolites can still be found today in Australia and North America.

EON	PRECAMBRIAN — FIRST LANDMASSES							
ERA				PALAEOZOIC — AGE OF ANCIENT LIFE				
PERIOD		CAMBRIAN	ORDOVICIAN	SILURIAN	DEVONIAN	CARBONIFEROUS		PERMIAN
EPOCH						MISSISSIPPIAN	PENNSYLVANIAN	
	4,560 million years ago (mya)	544 mya	495 mya	443 mya	417 mya	354 mya	323 mya	290 mya

◄ METEORITE CRATER
Mass extinctions occur in Earth's history when many life-forms die out at once. The age of dinosaurs may have been ended by a huge meteorite that struck the Yucatan peninsula in Mexico, 65 million years ago. Dust clouds rising from the impact would have blotted out the Sun's light for years, killing plants and dinosaurs.

◄ WOOLLY MAMMOTH
This mammoth calf was dug up in Siberia in 1977. It is not a fossil, but the whole animal. Ice in the frozen soil kept it from rotting when it died. Mammoths looked like elephants, but with more hair and smaller ears. They roamed the northern grasslands until a cooling climate and hunting by humans killed them off about 11,000 years ago.

FOSSIL RECORD
Fossils are an important tool for understanding Earth's history. They enable us to study extinct animals that lived a long time ago. Because rock layers from different periods contain different fossils, scientists can use fossils to discover how Earth has changed. This geologist is excavating a dinosaur fossil in the southwest United States.

HOMO SAPIENS SKULL
Human-like skulls and footprints found in Africa date back 4.5 million years. They suggest our ancestors were short, ape-like, and walked on hind legs. Modern humans – *Homo sapiens* – appeared just 130,000 years ago. If Earth's history to date were squeezed into one day, we arrived at two seconds to midnight!

JURASSIC FERNS
Ferns are ancient plants that date back more than 300 million years. This rainforest in Washington State has many ferns like those of the Jurassic period, when dinosaurs lumbered through ferny undergrowth to feed on cone-bearing and palm-like trees. There were, however, no flowering plants in the Jurassic period.

▲ GRAZING MAMMALS
Mammals took over when the dinosaurs died out. Their age, the Cenozoic era, began 65 million years ago and continues today. They inherited a cooler world with flowering plants and grasses. New kinds of mammals evolved to live on open plains. They had chopping and grinding teeth and legs designed for running.

PHANEROZOIC – AGE OF ABUNDANT EVIDENT LIFE											
MESOZOIC – AGE OF DOMINANT REPTILES				CENOZOIC – AGE OF DOMINANT MAMMALS							
TRIASSIC	JURASSIC	CRETACEOUS		TERTIARY					QUATERNARY		
		LOWER	UPPER	PALAEOCENE	EOCENE	OLIGOCENE	MIOCENE	PLIOCENE	PLEISTOCENE	HOLOCENE	
251 mya	206 mya	142 mya	99 mya	65 mya	55 mya	34 mya	24 mya	5.3 mya	1.8 mya	0.01 mya	Today

INSIDE THE EARTH

Earth is made up of different layers, which formed when the planet was young and extremely hot. The main layers are the core at the centre, then the mantle, and finally the crust on which we live. Earth is still very hot today. The heat creates flow in the inner molten rock layers, causing plates – pieces of the brittle crust – to slide about over them. Evidence of this active, changing planet can be seen at the surface: the movement of the plates creates volcanoes and earthquakes. In fact, it was through studying earthquake tremors that scientists discovered the existence of Earth's layers.

inside Earth

Upper mantle: partly molten rock, 670 km (416 miles) thick; temp. 1,000°C (1,800°F)

Lower mantle: solid rock, 2,230 km (1,385 miles) thick; temp. 3,500°C (6,300°F)

Outer core: liquid metals, about 2,250 (1,400 miles) thick; temp. 4,000°C (7,20

Inner core: solid metals, about 2,440 km (1515 m across; temp. 7,00 (12,600°F)

Oceanic crust: so basalt, 8 km (5 m thick; temp. up to 1,000°C (1,800°F)

Continental crust: s rock (various), up to 70 km (45 miles) thi temp. up to 1,000°C (1,800°F)

▲ EARTH'S LAYERS

Earth was originally a fusion of hot, molten gas and dust. Lighter elements floated to the surface and cooled to form the crust. Heavier elements, such as iron and nickel, sank to the core. Mantle rocks have a basalt-like composition. The upper mantle is near melting point and flows slowly. Greater pressure deepe down makes the lower mantle more solid. Likewise, metals are molten in the ou core, but are made solid in the inner core as a result of immense pressure.

▼ CRUSTAL LANDSCAPE FEATURES

The lithosphere is Earth's rigid shell, combining the crust with the uppermost mantle layer. It is broken into many separate plates. Heat from deep inside Earth creates currents in the mantle below, which cause the plates to slide around in different directions. In some places they collide head-on, and in others they grind alongside one another or drift apart.

MOLTEN IRON (CORE)
No samples of Earth's core have been studied, but it is thought to be made up mostly of iron, along with a little nickel. Both metals are very dense and heavy, and they sank beneath other materials early in Earth's history: the core was the first of the planet's layers to form. Today, iron makes up about 35% of Earth's total mass. Heat and planetary rotation make molten iron swirl around the outer core. This motion generates the planet's magnetic field.

PERIDOTITE (MANTLE)
Peridotite is a dark, heavy rock made mainly from olivine and pyroxene. Samples of the rock have been ejected from deep below ground during volcanic eruptions. They show that the mantle is made up of olivine and other minerals containing magnesium, iron, and silica. Scientists have squeezed olivine in the laboratory and found that its crystals pack more solidly under pressure, as seen in this microscopic close-up of a thin slice of peridotite.

BASALT (CRUST)
Basalt is a fine-grained, heavy volcanic rock. It is formed from magma that flows up from the mantle into gaps between diverging crustal plates. It is the most common rock on Earth's surface. Basalt can erupt on continents (as seen above in these basalt columnar formations) but it also forms the oceanic crust. No part of the basalt ocean floor is older than 200 million years, because the rock is constantly being consumed in subduction zones.

FEATURES OF THE EARTH'S CRUST

1. **Continental crust:** made up of various rock types, and thicker than oceanic crust
2. **Basin:** wide depressions formed in front of elevated areas and filled with sediment
3. **Colliding continental plates:** the crust is stacked up along faults
4. **Uplifted mountain range:** continental collision piles up rock to form high mountain range
5. **Oceanic crust:** several times thinner than continental crust, but made of heavier basalt
6. **Upper mantle:** partly molten; solid uppermost part combines with crust to form lithosphere
7. **Lower mantle:** solid, dense rock such as peridotite below the upper mantle
8. **Spreading oceanic plates:** as they move apart, lava rises to form a mid-oceanic ridge
9. **Mantle hot spot:** volcanoes form islands where magma rises from the mantle
10. **Trench:** created at subduction zone as oceanic plate sinks below lighter continental plate
11. **Subduction zone:** formed where plates converge and one sinks below the other
12. **Stratovolcano:** formed above subduction zone from magma generated in mantle below
13. **Rift valley:** crust pulls apart, and the land between drops, creating a valley

MOVING EARTH

The Earth is moving beneath our feet. Its hard shell, the lithosphere, is made up of the crust and the hard, uppermost part of the upper mantle. It is broken into 17 plates, which drift on the asthenosphere, the semi-molten part of the upper mantle. The word used to describe the movement of Earth's plates is tectonics. The plates beneath the oceans are quite thin but are made of heavy material, while continental plates are made from lighter, thicker material. Some plates are sliding past one another, some are coming together, and others are moving apart. The boundaries where plates meet are where many of Earth's most interesting features occur, in the form of mountain ranges, volcanoes, ocean trenches, and earthquakes.

tectonics

▼ CONVERGING PLATES: HIMALAYAS
The Himalaya mountains in central Asia were created when two continental plates converged, or collided. About 50 million years ago the plate carrying India drifted northeastwards into the Eurasian mainland. If it had been a heavy oceanic plate, it would have sunk beneath the Eurasian Plate. Since both plates were continental, they were too thick and light for one to sink beneath the other. The northern edge of the Indian Plate crumpled, pushing up the Himalayas.

Mountains formed by two continental plates colliding

Eurasian Plate

Indian Plate

PLATE BOUNDARIES

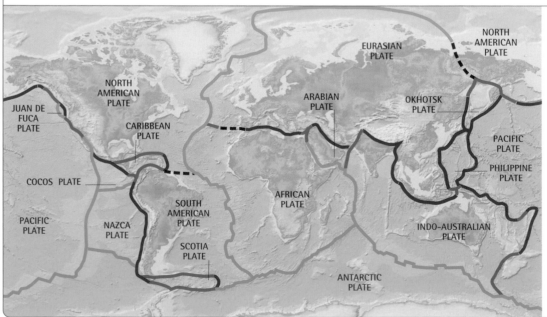

EURASIAN PLATE

NORTH AMERICAN PLATE

NORTH AMERICAN PLATE

JUAN DE FUCA PLATE

CARIBBEAN PLATE

ARABIAN PLATE

OKHOTSK PLATE

PACIFIC PLATE

PHILIPPINE PLATE

COCOS PLATE

AFRICAN PLATE

SOUTH AMERICAN PLATE

PACIFIC PLATE

NAZCA PLATE

SCOTIA PLATE

INDO-AUSTRALIAN PLATE

ANTARCTIC PLATE

Plate boundaries fall into three groups: convergent (moving together), divergent (moving apart), and transform (sliding past one another). The boundaries are where most of Earth's major earthquakes take place. Really big earthquakes are especially common along convergent and transform boundaries. Volcanoes are also common at the convergent boundaries around the Pacific coastline. Most divergent boundaries lie along mid-ocean ridges, where the gap they leave is plugged by basalt magma (molten rock) rising from the mantle below and cooling to form new solid crust on the ocean floor.

KEY TO MAP

——— *convergent boundary*

——— *divergent boundary*

——— *transform fault*

- - - - - *uncertain boundary*

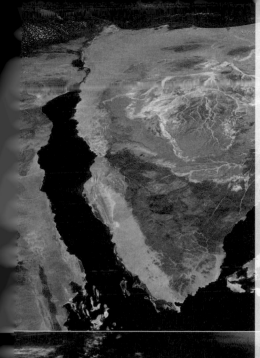

◄ DIVERGENT BOUNDARY

The Red Sea has divided East Africa and Arabia since the African and Arabian Plates began diverging some 50 million years ago. As the plates parted, great slabs of land slipped down into the gap in a series of faults. Later, the gap (or rift) filled with seawater. The Red Sea rift connects to the mid-ocean ridge of the Indian Ocean.

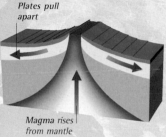

Plates pull apart

Magma rises from mantle

◄ CONVERGENT BOUNDARY

The Andes in South America form a volcanic mountain range created by subduction – an oceanic plate sinking under a continental plate at a convergent boundary. As the Nazca Plate went under the South American Plate, it sank into the mantle, causing parts of the overlying mantle to melt and form magma. The magma then rose through the crust to form volcanoes.

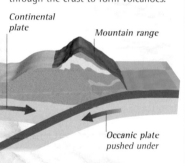

Continental plate

Mountain range

Oceanic plate pushed under

◄ TRANSFORM FAULT

The San Andreas Fault, on the US Pacific coast, marks a transform boundary. The Pacific and North American Plates are sliding past one another, but rock friction causes them to stick for long periods. Tension gradually builds up, and the sudden movement as they slip past one another creates a violent shock – an earthquake. A major earthquake on this fault, in 1906, caused fires that engulfed central San Francisco.

Earthquakes caused when two plates slip

MOVING CONTINENTS

The German geophysicist Alfred Wegener (1880–1930) was one of the first to suggest that continents moved. The opposing coastlines of the South Atlantic Ocean looked similar to him. He reasoned that the edges of the major landmasses could be put back together, like a jigsaw puzzle. His idea was not widely accepted until the 1960s.

PANGAEA

The plates of the lithosphere have been in motion since they first formed 3.5 billion years ago. These movements have brought continents together, split them apart, and reshaped oceans. Wegener's assembled jigsaw, named Pangaea, shows how the landmasses would have looked 200 million years ago, in the time of the early dinosaurs.

DRIFTING CONTINENTS

One hundred million years later, Pangaea lay in pieces. Divergent plates had begun to open up the Atlantic Ocean. South America was drifting west. Antarctica was heading for the South Pole. Off the eastern coast of Africa, India was creeping northeast towards Asia.

THE EARTH TODAY

Today's map shows India in place after it collided with the Eurasian mainland. Greenland has separated from North America, which now has a land bridge with South America. Australia has drifted into the Pacific. In 100 million years the map will look quite different.

PROOF OF SHIFTING PLATES ►

Rocks have provided evidence for the theory of Earth's moving plates. Fossils of *Glossopteris*, an ancient plant, had been found in India, Australia, Africa, and South America. These lands, now far apart, must have been joined 250 million years ago, in *Glossopteris's* day. Likewise, fossils of *Mesosaurus*, a freshwater reptile that lived 280 million years ago, have been found only on the Atlantic coasts of Africa and South America.

MESOSAURUS FOSSIL

Seed fern

GLOSSOPTERIS FOSSIL

EXPLODING EARTH

About four-fifths of Earth's total surface is volcanic rock. It rose through the crust as magma (molten rock) from the upper mantle, before emerging in the form of lava, which then cooled and hardened. Volcanoes are visible proof of an active, changing planet. They are most common at tectonic plate boundaries. Where two oceanic plates move apart, relatively gentle eruptions produce long volcanic ridges on the seafloor. But where an oceanic plate sinks beneath another plate, chains of stratovolcanoes form. Stratovolcanoes have highly explosive eruptions capable of causing widespread devastation.

e ▶▶
volcanoes

STRATOVOLCANO ▶

Magma rises through cracks and builds up in chambers. Eventually, pressure from below forces it up to the surface to erupt. Very runny lava, with a low gas and silica content, erupts in gushing rivers. Very sticky lava, with a high gas and silica content, erupts explosively. It blasts out pyroclastic materials (clouds of ash made up of powdered rock and fragments of volcanic glass) and blobs of lava. Explosive volcanoes that eject both pyroclastic materials and lava are called stratovolcanoes.

8
7
6
2
5
2
3
1

GLOBAL VOLCANIC ACTIVITY (FAMOUS VOLCANOES)

MOUNT ST HELENS
MOUNT VESUVIUS
MAUNA LOA
MOUNT PINATUBO
TAMBORA

NAME	MAJOR ERUPTION	PLACE
Mauna Loa	Continuous	Hawaii, USA
Mount Pinatubo	1991	Luzon, Philippines
Mount St Helens	1980	Washington, USA
Tambora	1815	Sundas, Indonesia
Mount Vesuvius	AD 79	Pompeii, Italy

▲ MOUNT ST HELENS, USA
Mount St Helens, USA, erupted with explosive force in 1980. This ancient stratovolcano had started showing signs of activity in March, in step with a series of earthquakes in the region. On 18 May, a quake triggered a massive landslide and Mount St Helens erupted. Almost 1 km³ (0.24 cu miles) of rock was blown into the air, and the peak was left shorter by 400 m (1,350 ft).

Shield volcano: runny lava produces gently sloping sides

▲ MAUNA LOA, HAWAII
Mauna Loa on Hawaii Island is the world's largest volcano, rising more than 17 km (11 miles) from its base. The volcanoes that make up the Hawaiian Island chain (most of which are underwater) stretch 2,400 km (1,500 miles) across the Pacific Ocean, and were formed as the Pacific Plate moved over a fixed "hot spot". It is a shield volcano, a gently sloping mound built up by repeated eruptions of runny lava. Unlike stratovolcanoes, shield volcanoes seldom erupt explosively.

STRATOVOLCANO

(1) **Asthenosphere:** lower layer of upper mantle containing partially molten rock
(2) **Lithosphere:** Earth's solid outer layer (crust combined with uppermost layer of the upper mantle)
(3) **Magma chamber:** a reservoir in the crust filled by rising magma from below
(4) **Pluton:** a buried mass of igneous rock that forms when magma in an old chamber cools and hardens
(5) **Pipe:** the vertical channel through the crust by which magma reaches the surface
(6) **Composite layers:** deposits of lava and pyroclastic material from earlier eruptions
(7) **Vent:** the opening at the surface from which volcanic materials are ejected; some volcanoes have several
(8) **Pyroclastic flow:** a hot – and deadly – cloud of ash and gases that flows very rapidly down the sides
(9) **Lava:** river of molten rock (magma is known as lava when it reaches the surface)
(10) **Caldera:** a crater that forms when the walls of the vent collapse, usually after a violent eruption

Fissure eruption: lava flows from opening due to weak crust

▲ PITON DE LA FOURNAISE, REUNION
The Piton de la Fournaise on Réunion Island is a basaltic volcano, formed by a hot spot, and one of the most active volcanoes on Earth, erupting roughly once every two years. Réunion Island forms the tip of a huge volcano rising from the ocean floor, which was created by a hot spot in the Indian Ocean off the east coast of Madagascar. During eruptions, fissure vents often open up on the flanks of Piton de la Fournaise, sending out fluid red-hot lava flows; the crusted black lava creeps along at a much slower rate.

RIVERS OF FIRE

Some volcanic eruptions are violent explosions of lava, gas, and ash. At the other extreme, the volcanoes on Hawaii pour out huge fountains and rivers of lava but cause little damage. What puts the bang in a volcano? The answer lies in the lava. The explosive form, known as rhyolitic or andesitic lava, is typically hot and sticky. It may contain many volatiles (dissolved gases) and silica. The lava on, for instance, Hawaii is of the basaltic form: very hot and runny, and relatively low in silica and volatiles.

e ▶▶ volcanoes

STROMBOLIAN ERUPTION ON MOUNT ETNA, SICILY
A Strombolian explosion is when a volcano repeatedly sends jets
fluid lava into the air, after the active volcano on Stromboli, an island o
Sicily. The gases released from volcanoes, such as steam and carbon dioxid
are called volatiles. While magma remains deep below ground, pressu
keeps the volatiles dissolved. As the magma rises, the pressure drops and tl
volatiles escape – similar to when you open a fizzy drink. The bubblir
volatiles blow the magma into fragments as it is ejected from the volcan

▼ **LAVA LAKE IN KILAUEA CRATER, HAWAII**
Kilauea on Hawaii is one of the most active and studied volcanoes in the world.
It is a typical shield volcano, whose shallow cone shape is built up from many
layers of basaltic lava produced by frequent but gentle eruptions, often from
several vents (openings) in the slopes and crater. Fluid lava is usually associated
with ocean floor and hot spot activity, such as that found under Hawaii. Basaltic
lava often spreads over a wide area before solidifying.

Caldera (sunken crater) filled with basaltic lava

Basaltic lava has low silica content but extremely high temperatures

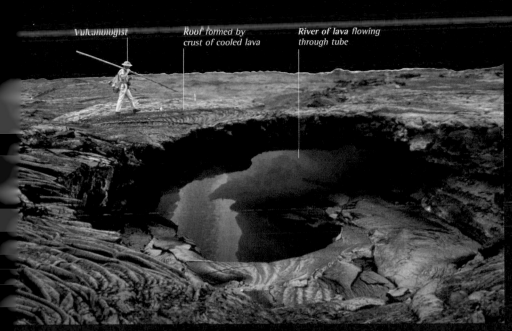

Volcanologist

Roof formed by crust of cooled lava

River of lava flowing through tube

◄ ROOFED LAVA TUBE, HAWAII

Lava tubes form from rivers of very hot and runny lava, usually the basaltic type. When lava flows down a narrow gulley, the skin on its surface may harden into a roof. Under the roof, a tube of hot lava continues to flow. Tube roofs frequently collapse in places, as this example on Hawaii has done. When lava tubes drain dry, they become volcanic caves that can be explored.

BASALT COLUMNS IN NAMIBIA ►

Basalt lava sometimes cools naturally into many-sided columns. This picture shows a volcanic rock formation from Twyfelfontein, Namibia, known as the "Organ Pipes", after their perpendicular shape and arrangement. These pillars, made from dolerite (a type of basalt), formed around 120 million year ago. Distinctive basalt columns can also be found on the northern coast of Ireland (the "Giant's Causeway") and in Iceland.

TYPES OF BASALT LAVA

PILLOW LAVA

When an underwater volcano erupts, it often creates pillow lava on the sea-bed. As lava comes into contact with the cold water it quickly forms a thick skin, which allows the lava inside each "pillow" to cool relatively slowly. If you find pillow lava on dry land it is a sure sign that the area once lay underwater.

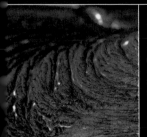

PAHOEHOE LAVA

Pahoehoe (pronounced "pah-hoy-hoy") is the Hawaiian word for "ropey". It is common in Hawaiian eruptions. This very fluid lava erupts in thin sheets that flow rapidly over large areas. It forms a smooth, stretchy skin that is drawn into rope-like folds and globules as the molten lava flows beneath it.

AA LAVA

Aa (pronounced "ah-ah") is another common form of Hawaiian lava. Cooler than pahoehoe, it is also sticky and slower-flowing. A thick skin forms, which crumbles as it oozes along. The slivers and chunks have dangerously jagged edges, which make it impossible to walk on in bare feet. This may explain how the lava got its name!

▲ GEOTHERMAL ENERGY, ICELAND

Natural hot springs are common in highly volcanic regions, where underground lakes of magma lie close to Earth's surface. As water seeps deep into the ground, it is heated by the magma and by the high pressure at great depths. It rises again as steam, shooting from the ground in scalding fountains called geysers or bubbling into mineral-rich lakes. This lake in Iceland doubles as a source of geothermal ("Earth-heated") energy and as a relaxing hotpool.

LIVING WITH VOLCANOES

Today, roughly half a billion people live near a volcano. Many of them risk being killed by an eruption or its after-effects. Why do they stay? One reason is that volcanic ash makes land fertile and good for farming. In any case, volcanoes may be dormant (inactive) for years between eruptions. Even so, scientists watch volcanoes carefully for warning signs of danger. Volcanoes can be the source of rivers of mud or of debris long after they have erupted, and over the last three centuries they have killed more than a quarter of a million people.

volcanoes

▲ MOUNT VESUVIUS
This is the bustling Bay of Naples today, with the volcanic Mount Vesuvius looming on the skyline. On 24 August, AD 79, the volcano erupted. A pyroclastic flow (a mass of gases and ash) raced down the slopes and buried the Roman towns of Pompeii and Herculaneum. The townsfolk were unprepared for the eruption, since Vesuvius had been dormant for centuries, and several thousand died, mostly from heat or choking. The next eruption may endanger as many as three million people.

▲ POMPEII
In Pompeii 2,000 people were buried by a layer of ash up to 30 m (100 ft) thick. The ash hardened into pumice, which preserved the shapes of the corpses. Plaster casts of the victims reveal their last moments.

▲ INDONESIA
Volcanic ash is not ash at all, but a fine powder made from tiny particles of rock and glass. After an eruption, it settles in layers and enriches the soil. The land surrounding the volcanoes of Indonesia is used for growing rice and other crops. The volcanoes lie beneath busy flight paths. Jets flying into a volcanic ash cloud from an eruption can have their engines badly damaged.

VOLCANO TIMELINE ▶
Scientists rate the power of a volcanic eruption on a scale called the Volcanic Explosivity Index. Luckily, super-volcanoes that score 8 or more are rare. The last one took place about 74,000 years ago in Sumatra.

SCORING ON THE VOLCANIC EXPLOSIVITY INDEX

Crater Lake, Oregon, USA	Kikai, Ryukyu Island, Japan	Santorini (Thera), Greece	Vesuvius, Italy
(7)	(7)	(6)	(7)
c. 4895 BC	c. 4350 BC	c. 1390 BC	AD 79

▲ GLOBAL SUNSCREEN
The explosion that rocked Mount Pinatubo was one of the largest eruptions of the 20th century. This satellite picture shows a vast plume of particles around the equator, 2 months after they were ejected 30 km (19 miles) into the atmosphere. They reflected the Sun's light and lowered the global temperature by 1°C (1.8°F).

▲ SEISMOMETER
A scientist sets up a seismograph to measure ground vibrations caused by volcanoes and earthquakes. Today seismologists monitor volcanoes that might erupt along busy flight paths, such as those over Alaska.

▲ PINATUBO
This strange scene was created by a shower of volcanic ash. In June 1991, Mount Pinatubo in the Philippines erupted in a titanic explosion, blowing more than 5 km³ (1.2 cu miles) of rock and volcanic ash into the air. The debris then fell back to Earth in waves of hot ash. Heavy rains fell and created lahars: sludgy rivers of mud, wet ash, and rock. The lahars streamed down valleys at speeds of up to 65 kph (40 mph), burying houses and killing people.

▲ LAHAR (MUD FLOW)
Rainfall on Mount Pinatubo is very heavy from June to September. For 4 years after the 1991 eruption, lahars flowed without warning into nearby towns. In all, more than 100,000 people have lost their homes.

6   7   6   6   7   7

raefajokull, Iceland 1362   Tambora, Indonesia 1815   Krakatau, Indonesia 1883   Katmai (Novarupta), Alaska 1912   Mount St Helens, USA 1980   Pinatubo, Philippines 1991

EARTHQUAKES

Earthquakes commonly occur along Earth's tectonic plate boundaries, where there are faults. Faults are fractures that develop where tectonic activity is pushing the rock on one side past the rock on the other. But friction makes the rocks along the fault stick, and they become stressed. When the stress overcomes the friction, the rocks move suddenly, causing an earthquake. Its size depends on how much energy is released. There are three main faults: strike-slip, normal, and reverse or thrust faults.

EARTHQUAKE ZONES (FEATURED EARTHQUAKES)

QUAKE SITE	DATE	RICHTER SCALE	DEATHS
Alaska, USA	1964	8.4	131
San Francisco, USA	1906	8.3	500+
Duzce, Turkey	1999	7.2	260
Kobe, Japan	1995	6.9	5,500
Northridge, USA	1994	6.7	51

▲ DUZCE, TURKEY (1999)
In 1999, an earthquake measuring 7.2 on the Richter Scale struck Turkey. Long faults make big earthquakes as they build up more stress along the length of the fault. The North Anatolian strike-slip fault in Turkey is more than 1,200 km (745 miles) long. Since 1939, there have been 11 large earthquakes on this fault.

▲ GRAND TETON MOUNTAINS, WYOMING, USA
Some landforms are created by earthquake movements. The mountains of Grand Teton National Park in Wyoming were created by movement along a normal fault, where the rock is being pulled apart. Rocks along the east side of the Teton fault line move downwards, leaving the opposing rock forming high mountains.

STRIKE-SLIP FAULT In strike-slip faults, ground movement is horizontal. In this right-lateral strike-slip, you would see the ground on the opposite side of the fault move to your right.

NORMAL FAULT In a normal fault, movement is caused by rock being pulled apart. The side above the fault line drops down – in this case in a near-vertical direction.

RICHTER SCALE
In 1935, American Charles Richter invented a scale for measuring the size, or magnitude, of earthquakes.

Generally not felt by people	Felt by few people	Felt by some: causes very little damage	Felt by most: causes little damage	Causes damaging shocks
❶	❷	❸	❹	❺

earthquakes

◄ SEWARD, ALASKA
This fishing boat was hurled from the water by a Pacific-wide tsunami generated by the great Alaskan earthquake of 1964. People died as far away as Newport Beach, California. Most of the damage and lives lost from this earthquake were due to the effects of these giant water waves, created either by the movements of the ocean floor or by underwater landslides in nearby bays. Tsunamis can cross the ocean at speeds of up to 950 kph (600 mph) and reach fearsome heights of up to 30 m (100 ft) by the time they hit the coast.

▲ NORTHRIDGE, LOS ANGELES (1994)
Although the Northridge earthquake of 1994 was considered moderate, measuring only 6.7 on the Richter Scale, it was the most costly earthquake in US history. It was caused by movement on a thrust fault. Loss of life was minimized by strict building codes and the early morning hour of the quake.

REVERSE OR THRUST FAULT In reverse faults, caused by rocks being compressed, the side above the fault moves up. They are called thrust faults if, as here, the dip or angle of the fault is low.

uctive in populated reas

Major earthquake: can cause serious damage

Great earthquake: can destroy towns over a wide area

⑦　　　⑧　　　⑨

▲ ALASKA, 1964
The 1964 Alaska earthquake was the second largest ever recorded, measuring 8.4 on the Richter Scale and lasting 4 minutes. On the modern earthquake measure, the Moment Magnitude Scale, it registered 9.2. The largest recorded earthquake (Richter 8.6, MM 9.5) struck Chile in 1960.

STUDYING EARTHQUAKES

What makes an earthquake destructive? The answer lies in the seismic shockwaves it sends out. There are different types of waves. Surface waves ripple along Earth's surface. These waves cause the most damage. Other waves, known as body waves, travel through Earth's interior. Seismic waves can be detected far away by sensitive vibration recorders called seismographs. Seismologists – scientists who study earthquakes – are still learning about Earth's interior and how earthquakes occur. A better understanding of why and when earthquakes happen can help to save lives in the future.

P-WAVES AND S-WAVES

Earthquakes send two kinds of body wave: P (primary) and S (secondary). P-waves push and pull like a concertina. S-waves "waggle" from side to side, like a rope. Both waves take curving paths, because they are bent by the differing densities they pass through. S-waves do not pass through the outer core, because they cannot travel through a liquid. Seismologists know how fast the waves travel, and that P-waves are nearly twice as fast as S-waves. They use seismographs of body waves to find out where earthquakes have occurred.

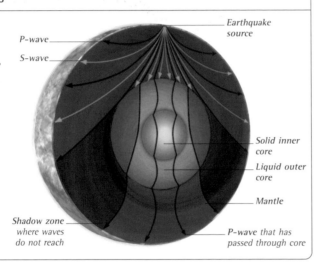

- P-wave
- S-wave
- Earthquake source
- Solid inner core
- Liquid outer core
- Mantle
- Shadow zone where waves do not reach
- P-wave that has passed through core

earthquakes

KOBE EARTHQUAKE ▶
On 17 January, 1995, an earthquake hit the large city of Kobe in Japan. Earthquakes are common in Japan, which lies near the boundary between 3 tectonic plates. But the Kobe region had shown few warning tremors, and the city was unprepared. For example, some districts were built on soft, wet sand instead of rock. When wet sand is shaken violently, it flows like a liquid. At Kobe, about 100,000 buildings collapsed and 5,500 people died.

PREDICTING EARTHQUAKES

ANCIENT CHINESE SEISMOGRAPH
In AD 132, the Chinese philosopher Chang Heng invented an earthquake detector. It was a large vase with 8 dragons' heads attached. Each dragon held a ball in its jaws, and beneath each head sat a cup in the shape of a toad with its mouth open. Any earthquake within a range of about 640 km (400 miles) would cause a ball to fall into a cup. The direction of the quake determined which ball would fall, so rescue parties would know where to go.

Dragon's head

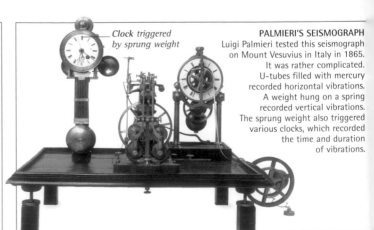

Clock triggered by sprung weight

PALMIERI'S SEISMOGRAPH
Luigi Palmieri tested this seismograph on Mount Vesuvius in Italy in 1865. It was rather complicated. U-tubes filled with mercury recorded horizontal vibrations. A weight hung on a spring recorded vertical vibrations. The sprung weight also triggered various clocks, which recorded the time and duration of vibrations.

◄ TURKEY EARTHQUAKE
This picture shows the extensive damage caused by an earthquake that struck the Turkish town of Duzce on 12 November, 1999. Three months earlier, another earthquake had struck the nearby city of Izmit, killing 18,000 people. Turkey sits on a major fault in Earth's crust. Each new tremor releases stress along a part of the fault. Seismologists believe that Ankara, the Turkish capital, will be hit before 2030.

5-SECOND UNITS

Earthquake epicentre

Coloured bands show 10 cm (4 in) of ground movement

▲ KOBE SEISMOGRAM
This is a seismogram of the 1995 Kobe earthquake. The horizontal scale records time: the gap between each vertical line represents 5 seconds. The zigzag line shows how much the ground is moving, measured in millimetres against the vertical scale. The small zigzags at the left are a jumble of secondary and surface waves. The longest ones are all surface waves, taking up a total of about 20 seconds. These are the waves that caused most of the damage on the ground.

OBSERVATORY
Modern seismographs are based around the mechanism of a pendulum – a heavy weight on a spring hanging from a support. During an earthquake, everything shakes except the pendulum. In early seismographs, a pencil attached to the stationary weight drew zigzags on a rotating drum of paper, as the paper moved with the vibrations. The zigzags showed how much the ground was shaking. Today's readings are taken with more sophisticated electronic instruments.

SATELLITE IMAGE OF EARTHQUAKE ▲
A coloured satellite radar picture shows an earthquake zone in California, USA, in 1999. The coloured bands are contours, each indicating 10 cm (4 in) of ground displacement, increasing towards the fault (upper centre). The earthquake measured 7.1 on the Richter Scale. Radar measurements were taken before and after the event by a European Remote Sensing (ERS-2) satellite and the information was then incorporated into this image.

SAN ANDREAS FAULT

The San Andreas Fault in western California is probably the best-studied fault in the world. It is part of a boundary between two tectonic plates, and frequent earthquakes have been shaking the region for nearly 30 million years. The fault came to scientists' attention after 1906, when a major earthquake left San Francisco in ruins and hundreds of people dead. Since then, more earthquakes along the fault have claimed lives. But progress has been made, too, in designing stronger buildings, so that if – or when – the next "Big One" hits California, people will be better prepared.

FAULT LINE

The fault runs along coastal California for about 1,300 km (800 miles). Two plates are slipping jerkily past one another at about 25 mm (1 in) a year. Parts of the fault move little but often, causing frequent medium-sized tremors. Other sections can stick for up to 300 years, storing up energy. When these finally slip, the result is a major earthquake.

NORTH AMERICA

PACIFIC OCEAN

COASTAL CALIFORNIA (CLOSE-UP BELOW)

San Andreas Fault

San Francisco

Los Angeles

North American Plate moving south

Northern Pacific Plate moving north

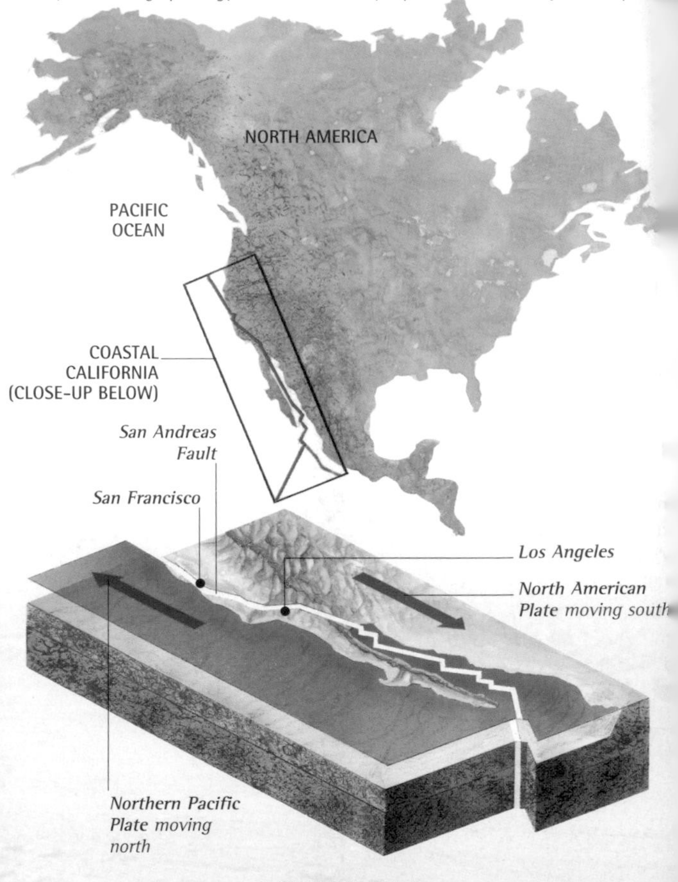

CLOSE-UP OF FAULT

Fault line

▲ SAN ANDREAS FAULT
An aerial view shows the San Andreas Fault as an unmistakable scar across the land. If you stand at ground level, facing the fault, and look across, you can see that ridges and gullies no longer match up with each other. Whichever side you are on, the opposite landmarks lie to the right of where they used to be. Geologists call this type of fault a right-lateral, strike-slip fault.

...REAT FIRE OF 1906

...18 April, 1906, a quake
...ng about 45 seconds
...ok the northern end of
... San Andreas Fault. In
...es the two sides of the
...t moved up to 6.4 m
...ft) past each other. In San
...ncisco, broken gas pipes
...ted several fires among the
...'s old, wooden buildings.
... blaze raged for three days.
...efighters were helpless
...ause their water supplies
...d been disrupted.

earthquakes

1933 LONG BEACH QUAKE

Disaster struck California again
in March 1933, in the form of
an earthquake at Long Beach.
Here, firefighters try to put out
the resulting fire at the Dodge
Tire Factory. Unlike the 1906
earthquake, which caused a
fire that burned on and on and
devastated San Francisco, the
1933 earthquake was tidied up
quickly by the fire services.

1989 DAMAGED BRIDGES

The 1989 earthquake struck
in a remote mountain range
100 km (60 miles) south of San
Francisco, but the city did not
escape damage. A double-deck
motorway collapsed, crushing
the cars below. The quake
killed more than 60 people,
but the toll would have been
higher without the lessons
learned from earlier disasters.

◄ JAPANESE PAGODA

Cedar ... re pole ... is main support

Loose, ... ay- tiled ... ofs move ... if shaken

For more than 1,400 years the Japanese have
built pagodas to survive earthquakes. Each
storey has heavy, clay-tiled roofs that are
fitted loosely to the building, and a strong
cedar pole stands at the centre. When hit by
an earthquake, the whole building wobbles
and sways with it instead of breaking apart.
The pole bends in a wave motion, but the
weight of the roofs acting against
one another cancels out the
waves and keeps the pole stable.

TRANSAMERICA BUILDING ►

Pyramid shape allows light to street below, and also makes building more stable

San Francisco's tallest building,
at 258 m (845 ft), is the
Transamerica Pyramid, built in
1972. Its deep concrete-and-
steel foundation, laid on rock,
is designed to move with an
earthquake, and the base
stands on a network of
stiltlike beams that can
cope with twisting
movements. During the
1989 earthquake, the top of
the building swayed by as
much as 30 cm (12 in) but it
suffered no damage.

LASER MONITORING OF GROUND MOVEMENT ▲

A researcher adjusts an experimental laser unit in the southern
Sierra Nevada region of California, a highly active area where
earthquakes are common. Lasers can detect movements
in Earth's surface as small as a hair's breadth. This type of
system may one day serve as an early warning system of major
earthquakes. Space scientists are also using the latest satellite
technology to track ground movements on Earth.

MOUNTAIN BUILDING

Mountains form where tectonic plates converge. The largest peaks form where continental plates collide and stack up layers of Earth's crust. Plate boundaries can produce long mountain systems called ranges. The highest, most rugged ranges are usually the youngest – they are on active plates and are often still growing. Older ranges are lower, with gentler slopes. The key process in mountain building is the deformation of rock by folding (caused by rock layers bending under pressure) and faulting (when the pressure forces the rock to fracture). Volcanic activity, which is common where continental and oceanic plates converge, also plays a part.

WORLD'S MOUNTAIN RANGES

HIGHEST MOUNTAINS	CONTINENT	HEIGHT
Everest (Sagarmatha)	Asia	8,850 m (29,035 f
Aconcagua	S America	6,960 m (22,835 f
Mount McKinley	N America	6,195 m (20,322 f
Kilimanjaro	Africa	5,965 m (18,980 f
Mount Elbrus	Europe	5,642 m (18,510 ft

Mountain ridge formed from deformed sedimentary rock

MOUNT KAGBENI, HIMALAYAS ▶
The Himalayas are Earth's biggest mountain range. They include 96 of the world's 100 highest peaks, including the 8,850-m (29,030-ft) Mount Everest (Sagarmatha). They began forming when two continental plates collided 50 million years ago. The Indian Plate crumpled, pushing rock upwards, and the range is still growing today.

Second Z-shape fold begins to form *First fo become m deform*

Sedimentary layers are laid down

SAND MODELS SHOWING TWO STAGES OF MOUNTAIN FORMATION

mountains

MODELLING MOUNTAINS ▶
We can replicate one way in which mountains are formed using sand models. A paper sheet is slowly rolled underneath layers of coloured sand. The paper creates friction under the sand, and folds start to develop. The more the paper is moved, the more folds are formed. Eventually, when the compressed rock cannot fold any more it fractures, creating fault lines. The final set of folds represents the newest mountain ranges.

Simple deformation of sedimentary rock *Foothills* *Rocks fracture (fault) under pressure* *Fold mountains created by repeated faulting and folding*

◄ SIERRA NEVADA

The 565-km (350-mile) long Sierra Nevada range, which lies inland from the California coast, was formed by volcanic activity. As the Pacific Plate converged with the North American Plate and sank below it, rising magma was forced into Earth's crust. The magma pushed up through the crust and cooled into a belt of granite. Faults tilted the range to the west, creating the present Sierra Nevada.

Granite cools very slowly, allowing the crystals inside to grow large enough to be easily seen

BANDED GRANITE ►

Granite rock makes up the backbone of the Sierra Nevada range. After a period of volcanic activity which ended about 80 million years ago, millions of years of glacial uplift and erosion wore away other volcanic rock, exposing the granitic core of the range and forming scenic features such as the Yosemite Valley.

◄ CHUGACH

The Chugach mountains follow the coastline of southern Alaska for 600 km (373 miles). As the Pacific Plate sank beneath the North American Plate, sedimentary rock was scraped off the sinking oceanic plate, folded and heaped up, and added onto the western edge of the American continent.

Ammonite fossils over 180 million years old

SEASHELLS IN ROCK ►

Geologists study fossils to learn how rocks formed. Ancient seashells in mountains show that these rocks came from the sea-bed. Fossils of sea life are found at high elevations in most mountain ranges. Fine-grained sedimentary rocks are one of the best types for preserving fossils.

Young peaks are still rising

Ancient slopes have been levelled by erosion

▲ MOUNT ST ELIAS, ALASKA

Mount St Elias on the southern coast of Alaska rises to 5,489 m (18,008 ft) from sea level. This spectacular mountain was created by tectonic activity in the last few million years. It is still growing today, and rapidly moving glaciers erode the peak as it rises.

▲ APPALACHIANS, USA

Formed before North America and Europe separated, the Appalachians in the eastern USA are among the world's oldest mountains. Several hundred million years ago they were a range of high, pointed peaks, but constant erosion has worn them down to gentle slopes.

MOUNTAIN WEATHER CONDITIONS

Great mountain ranges have a significant effect on the local climate. For example, the Andes mountains in South America create a massive barrier to moisture-laden winds blowing west. The peaks push up the air, which then drops its rain on the eastern slopes. Meanwhile, the western slopes are left dry. Similarly, the Himalayas cause monsoon winds to drop rain on the southern foothills; some villages in northeast India have an annual rainfall of more than 11 m (35 ft).

LANDSLIDES

A landslide is the sudden downward sliding of a mass of unstable material such as rock or soil. It is just one of the ways that a large mass of land material can move. In this case, it moves under the influence of gravity. A mass becomes unstable when it slopes too steeply, absorbs too much water, or is changed by the effects of weathering and erosion. Landslides can be triggered by natural events, such as earthquakes, or by human activities, such as road construction or quarrying. Some mass movements are so slow that they are barely noticeable, while others occur with deadly speed, sweeping over homes and people.

ROCKSLIDE ▶
Rockslides, common in high mountain ranges, occur when the angle of a slope is too great for the layers of rock to hold together. A slope may become unstable in spring after melted snow seeps into the rock, or when river water has eroded rock at the base. Water makes the natural boundaries between the different rock layers more slippery. The friction between the layers decreases and the upper layers begin to slide.

Soil creep is imperceptible – the topsoil moves downhill 10 mm (0.4 in) a year

Slumping occurs when large slabs slip down vertically

Debris flow is likely when rain soaks a previously dry area, turning everything to mud

Rockfalls are the free movement of frost- or rain-loosened rock pieces

Bent telegraph poles indicate soil creep

◀ LANDSLIDE TYPES
Geologists describe mass movements according to material, type of motion, and speed. Soil creep describes how minute shifts among soil particles cause slow movement. Slumping is a faster movement in which slices of land slip down a concave slope. In a debris flow, a water-soaked mass of rocks or soil moves fast like a liquid. Rockfalls, caused by rock weathering, are rapid and direct.

▲ MOUNT HUASCARÁN: LANDSCAPE BEFORE LANDSLIDE

Mass movements can travel unbelievably quickly. This picture of Mount Huascarán in the Peruvian Andes shows the scene before an earthquake struck on 31 May, 1970. The tremor dislodged a small amount of ice from the high, steep peak. The ice collapsed onto rocky slopes below. As the materials mingled, they gathered momentum, forming a massive debris avalanche.

▲ MOUNT HUASCARÁN: LANDSCAPE AFTER LANDSLIDE

This was the scene of devastation after the debris avalanche from Mount Huascarán. More than 50 million m³ (65 million cubic yards) of rock, ice, and mud tumbled downhill at speeds up to 435 kph (270 mph). The tide of debris travelled 16 km (10 miles) downwards, wiping out entire communities, including the village of Yungay, and killing more than 17,000 people.

▲ MUDSLIDE CAUSED BY HEAVY RAINS

Catastrophic mudslides such as this one in Caracas, Venezuela, in 1999, can occur in dry regions after sudden, heavy rainfall. Plant roots help to hold soil down, and there is a higher risk when farmers have cleared forested hillsides and left topsoil exposed. Because there is little vegetation to anchor the ground surface, water flushes the loose topsoil into stream gullies. The sloppy mixture of water and mud flows downhill, carrying away rocks, trees, and even cars and houses.

landslides

◄ MAKING SLOPES UNSTABLE

In 1995, a section of hillside slumped onto the Californian town of La Conchita. Luckily, no one was killed, although 9 houses were flattened. An investigation revealed that very high rains had left the hillside waterlogged and unstable. A law of landslides is that any slope will continue to settle until it finds its angle of repose – that is, the steepest angle at which the slope is stable. At La Conchita, the waterlogging had changed the hillside's angle of repose.

LANDSLIDES CAUSED BY SEAS AND RIVERS

The crashing of waves on this coastal cliff has eaten away at the rock at the base. The rock above the area of erosion now has no support. It becomes unstable and eventually topples. The eroded cliff edge is now getting dangerously close to the houses. Something similar happens with rivers, where constant steady erosion can make the riverbanks unstable. Brief but heavy rainfall can cause flash floods, causing steep riverbanks to collapse and destroy bridges and houses.

ROCKS

The rock that makes up the crust of Earth is constantly changing. Under the ground it is melted by heat and squeezed by pressures from deep within Earth. On the surface it is weathered by frost, wind, and water. Every form of rock can be classed in one of three groups – sedimentary, igneous, or metamorphic – depending on how it was formed and what changes it has undergone. Rock is changed or broken down by forces such as heat, pressure, and erosion, and turned by these forces into a new form of rock. This continual process is known as the rock cycle.

◄ YOSEMITE VALLEY
Every rock, no matter how hard, suffers weathering and erosion when it is exposed on Earth's surface. This outcrop of jointed rock in Yosemite National Park is being splintered by "frost wedging", which occurs when water freezes and then expands, causing great damage to the rock that surrounds it.

rocks

UPPER CRUST

SEDIMENTARY
Sediments deposited by water gradually build up in layers – layering is a feature of sediments and the rocks they form. Older, deeper layers are squeezed under the weight above them. They become compacted. The sediment has now become lithified: it is solid rock.

CONGLOMERATE
Formed from large pebbles, conglomerate was originally deposited by flowing water.

CHALK
Chalk is a form of soft limestone, made from tiny fossilised algae cells.

CRUST

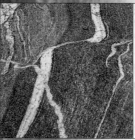

IGNEOUS
Igneous rocks begin life as magma – rock heated in Earth's mantle until it is molten. When magma rises through the crust, it cools and crystallizes into new rock. The slower the process, the larger the crystal and the coarser the rock. Granite, for example, contains large mineral crystals that grew slowly.

PORPHYRY
Large crystals within a mass of finer grains are characteristic of this rock.

BASALT
Dark and fine-grained, basalt is the most common igneous rock in Earth's crust.

DEEPER CRUST

METAMORPHIC
Metamorphic rocks have been transformed from one form to another by heat or pressure, for example, by deep volcanic heat or by the stresses of mountain building. Some metamorphic rocks take on a flaky or layered structure when put under pressure. Others recrystallize altogether.

SLATE
Slate is produced by the metamorphosis of the sedimentary rock shale.

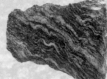

GNEISS
The metamorphis of silica-rich rocks, such as granite, creates this rock.

EROSION

...osion and weathering are a key part of the rock ...le. The exposed rock on these mountains is ...nstantly being weathered by frost wedging and ...ded by water. The smaller the rock fragment, the ...re easily it is moved. Rainwater washes the debris ...wn the lower slopes. On many high mountain ranges, ...aciers scour deep U-shaped valleys through the rock, ...rrying the loose debris downhill with them. When the ...bris is deposited over a large flat plain, as shown here, ...is known as an alluvial fan.

◄ DEPOSITION

Every year, some 36,000 km³ (8,636 cu miles) of water runs off the land into the oceans, carrying eroded material from surface rocks. Mud, silt, sand, and gravel are carried by flowing rivers. Along the way, some sediments are deposited on riverbeds and basins, such as these sediment plumes being deposited in the glacier-fed Peyto Lake in Alberta, Canada. Others end up on the margins of continents, where they build up to form sedimentary rock.

...HALE
...is rock is a mixture of clay ...inerals with particles of ...uartz, feldspar, and mica.

SANDSTONE
Quartz makes up the majority of this largely medium-grained, common rock.

...BSIDIAN
...hen lava cools quickly it ...roduces the glassy texture ...f rocks such as obsidian.

GABBRO
This is a hard rock that crystallizes underground over millions of years.

GRANITE
Known for its hardness, granite contains large crystals of quartz.

GARNET SCHIST
The term schist is used to describe a layered structure in metamorphic rock.

MIGMATITE
This rock is produced deep in the crust. It often contains bands of melted granite.

SIERRA NEVADA ►
Granite forms the foundation of many mountain ranges. Volcanic activity results in massive bodies of granite forming deep within Earth's crust. Granite bodies larger than 100 km² (40 sq miles) are known as batholiths. Batholiths can be found in the Sierra Nevada and parts of the Rockies.

MINERALS AND CRYSTALS

More than 4,000 minerals are known. Some are very rare, while a small handful make up most of the rocks in Earth's crust. Geologists define a mineral as a naturally occurring inorganic solid, with atoms arranged in an orderly pattern. Minerals that grow in unconstrained environments develop regular forms and are called crystals. Minerals are mined from Earth for many uses. Some minerals occur as a single pure element, but most are compounds (a combination) of elements.

◀ GRANITE
Granite is an igneous rock that cools slowly underground. The slow cooling allows the mixture of minerals within to form large, easily visible crystals and give the rock its coarse-grained texture. Granite varies in colour according to its mineral content: feldspar accounts for the pinkish tint, the greyish crystals are quartz, and the black specks are biotite.

BIOTITE   **QUARTZ**   **FELDSPAR**

Spring water is heated to about 70°C (160°F) before it emerges from rocks

COPPER

◀ COPPER MINE, ARIZONA
Humans first worked copper into tools at least 8,000 years ago, and the metal is still much used today. It is an element that sometimes occurs freely as a metal, but is more usually found mixed with other elements in sulphide or oxide minerals. Rocks that contain enough metal-bearing minerals are known as ore. Copper is extracted from ores that contain as little as 0.5% metal, so large amounts of ore must be mined to produce it.

OTHER PRECIOUS METALS

SILVER
A rare and precious metal, silver was used in the earliest coins. Although it occurs in a native state, it is more common in compounds. Mexico, Peru, and South Africa contain important silver mines, although 75% of the silver produced each year is a byproduct of the refining of gold, copper, zinc, and lead ores.

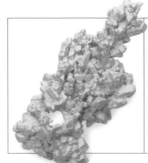

GOLD
Beautiful, and easily worked, gold has been sought after since earliest times. The metal exists almost entirely in a native state. It is found in rock veins or stream-beds, where it is washed after the weathering of gold-bearing rocks. Today, South Africa, Russia, and North America are the world's leading suppliers.

Pillow-like formations give Pammukale ("cotton castle") its name

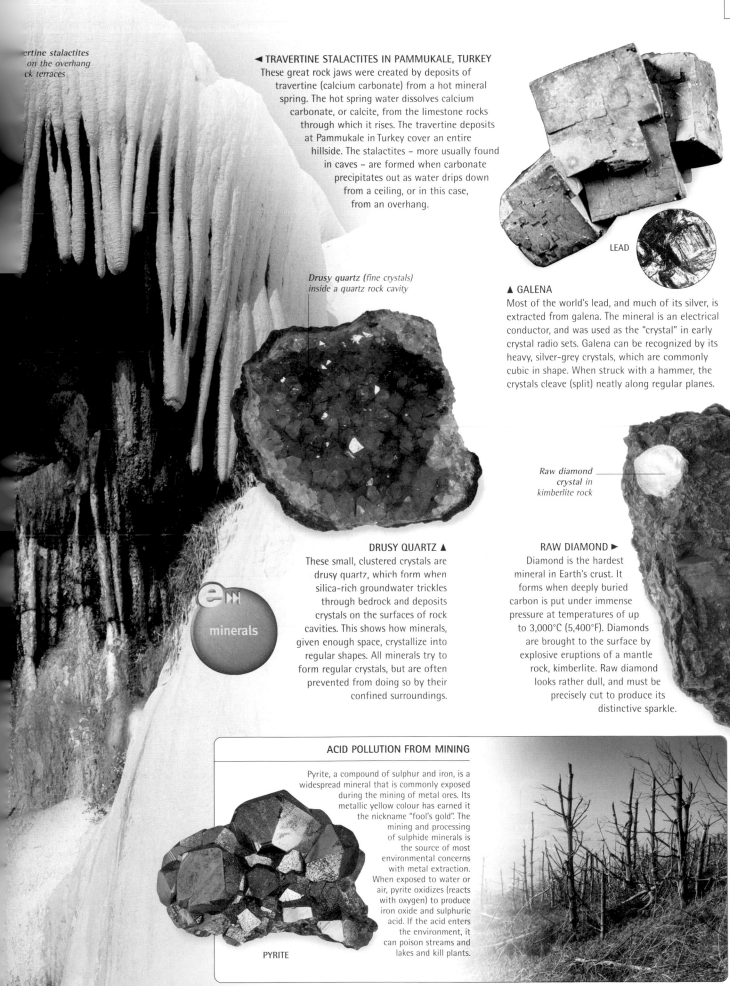

_ertine stalactites
on the overhang
ck terraces_

◄ TRAVERTINE STALACTITES IN PAMMUKALE, TURKEY
These great rock jaws were created by deposits of
travertine (calcium carbonate) from a hot mineral
spring. The hot spring water dissolves calcium
carbonate, or calcite, from the limestone rocks
through which it rises. The travertine deposits
at Pammukale in Turkey cover an entire
hillside. The stalactites – more usually found
in caves – are formed when carbonate
precipitates out as water drips down
from a ceiling, or in this case,
from an overhang.

LEAD

▲ GALENA
Most of the world's lead, and much of its silver, is
extracted from galena. The mineral is an electrical
conductor, and was used as the "crystal" in early
crystal radio sets. Galena can be recognized by its
heavy, silver-grey crystals, which are commonly
cubic in shape. When struck with a hammer, the
crystals cleave (split) neatly along regular planes.

_Drusy quartz (fine crystals)
inside a quartz rock cavity_

_Raw diamond
crystal in
kimberlite rock_

DRUSY QUARTZ ▲
These small, clustered crystals are
drusy quartz, which form when
silica-rich groundwater trickles
through bedrock and deposits
crystals on the surfaces of rock
cavities. This shows how minerals,
given enough space, crystallize into
regular shapes. All minerals try to
form regular crystals, but are often
prevented from doing so by their
confined surroundings.

minerals

RAW DIAMOND ►
Diamond is the hardest
mineral in Earth's crust. It
forms when deeply buried
carbon is put under immense
pressure at temperatures of up
to 3,000°C (5,400°F). Diamonds
are brought to the surface by
explosive eruptions of a mantle
rock, kimberlite. Raw diamond
looks rather dull, and must be
precisely cut to produce its
distinctive sparkle.

ACID POLLUTION FROM MINING

Pyrite, a compound of sulphur and iron, is a
widespread mineral that is commonly exposed
during the mining of metal ores. Its
metallic yellow colour has earned it
the nickname "fool's gold". The
mining and processing
of sulphide minerals is
the source of most
environmental concerns
with metal extraction.
When exposed to water or
air, pyrite oxidizes (reacts
with oxygen) to produce
iron oxide and sulphuric
acid. If the acid enters
the environment, it
can poison streams and
lakes and kill plants.

PYRITE

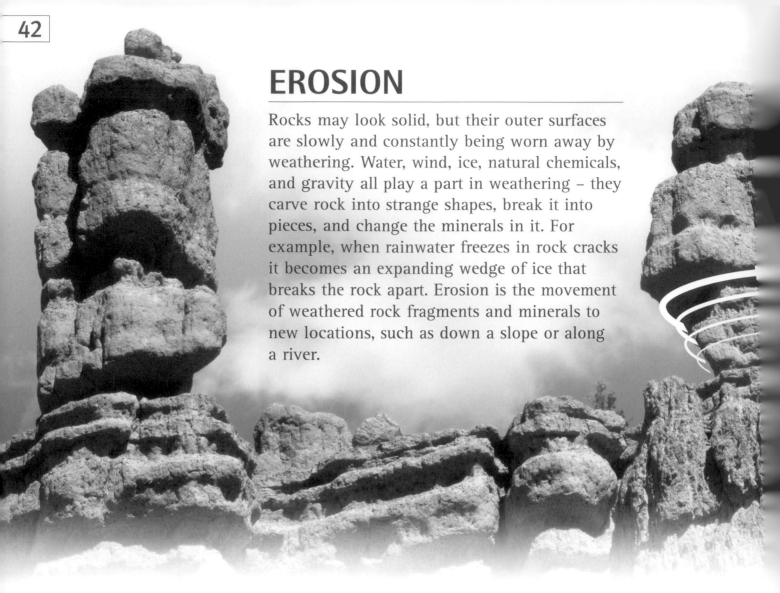

EROSION

Rocks may look solid, but their outer surfaces are slowly and constantly being worn away by weathering. Water, wind, ice, natural chemicals, and gravity all play a part in weathering – they carve rock into strange shapes, break it into pieces, and change the minerals in it. For example, when rainwater freezes in rock cracks it becomes an expanding wedge of ice that breaks the rock apart. Erosion is the movement of weathered rock fragments and minerals to new locations, such as down a slope or along a river.

Granite mountains at Yosemite stand 1,000 m (3,300 ft) tall

Sandstone pinnacles left by erosion

▲ **EXFOLIATED GRANITE OUTCROP AT YOSEMITE**
Outcrops of granite tower over the landscape of Yosemite National Park in California. The granite, a hard igneous rock, formed millions of years ago deep within Earth's crust. The rock overlying the granite has been eroded over the years. Freed from the pressure of the overlying rock, the granite begins to crack into layers like an onion. This is known as exfoliation. Water freezing in the cracks helps to separate the layers.

▲ **HOODOO LANDSCAPE AT BRYCE CANYON**
It is hard to believe that Bryce Canyon in Utah was once a solid plateau of sedimentary rock. Frosts have helped sculpt it into an eerie forest of towering hoodoos up to 60 m (200 ft) high. About 35 million years ago, the plateau was pushed up by forces in Earth's crust. It split into rows of rock walls divided by deep cracks. The walls were weathered by frost into fins, jagged blades, and finally hoodoos. Rains running off the land flush away the rock fragments.

HOODOOS

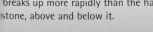

...e hoodoos (rock pillars) are all that remain of the upper ...s of a sedimentary rock plateau that has been weathered ... Cracks, opened up by rainwater and frost, have formed ...een each sedimentary layer in the hoodoos. The different ...layers weather away at different rates. The slender "necks" ...e hoodoos are made of a soft rock, such as mudstone. ...breaks up more rapidly than the harder rocks, such as ...stone, above and below it.

erosion

Slender neck of soft rock is worn away by wind action

Cracks between rock layers opened by frost wedging and chemical erosion

CHEMICAL EROSION

ERODED LIMESTONE
Rainwater causes chemical erosion in limestone. The water reacts with carbon dioxide in the air to become weakly acidic. The acid reacts with the rock to dissolve the mineral calcite. The water then carries the calcite away. After a long period, this process of erosion etches deep grooves in the surface of the rock.

KARST LANDSCAPE IN CHINA
These outcrops of limestone in China have been eroded by acidic rainwater into a range of sharp blade-like rocks. Landscapes like this are known as karst terrain. The same process of chemical erosion is at work here as in the photograph on the left; it has simply reached a much more advanced stage.

Limestone arch formed by wave action on surrounding softer rock

◄ V-SHAPED VALLEY
Fast-flowing rivers carve V-shaped valleys as they rush down steep hills. At the Lower Falls on Yellowstone River in Wyoming, the rock walls are almost sheer: the water is downcutting (eroding its bed) faster than the walls are being weathered. The stream passes over different rocks on its way down: the waterfalls are caused by a shelf of hard rock that is resistant to erosion.

U-SHAPED VALLEY ►
Glaciers, or rivers of ice, create a trademark U-shaped valley in mountains. Boulders gripped in the moving bed of ice grind against the rock walls and erode them. This is a hanging valley: the end of one glacial valley opening halfway up the side of another, deeper valley that cuts across it.

▲ COASTAL EROSION
Durdle Door is a natural rock arch on the Dorset coast in Britain. Set in a wall of two different limestones, the arch formed after the battering of sea waves eroded a panel of softer limestone. The cliffs to either side of the wall are made of even softer rocks. They have eroded much faster than the limestone, and the sea has worn away the coastline to make deep bays. The name of the arch comes originally from "thirl", an ancient English word meaning "pierced".

ISLANDS

Islands are landmasses surrounded by water. They are found inland, surrounded by lakes and rivers, and offshore, surrounded by seas and oceans. Offshore islands fall into two broad types: continental and oceanic. The first kind lie on the shallow, flooded margins of continents, and are simply outlying parts of the larger landmass. Oceanic islands are created from the seafloor, quite often in mid-ocean, by volcanic and tectonic activity. Many islands are home to fascinating plants and animals that have arrived from elsewhere and changed in unique ways to suit their new land. The same is true of the humans who have populated the islands of the world.

FLOODED MARGINS
Some islands are simply non-
submerged parts of nearby
continents. During the last Ic
Age, dry land connected the
British Isles to western Europ
Mammoth, elk, and Stone Ag
human hunters used the land
bridge. But the climate warm
sea levels rose, and by about
years ago the islands were cu

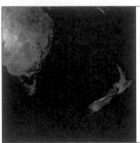

DIVERGING PLATES
New Zealand originated on th
east side of Australia. Starting
about 85 million years ago, rif
and seafloor spreading opened
and widened the Tasman Sea,
carrying New Zealand east and
separating it from Australia.
Since this time, New Zealand h
been an island with its own
geological history.

BORNEO
MINDANAO
(PHILLIPPINES)
IRIAN JAYA
JAVA
CELEBES
TIMOR

▲ INDONESIAN ARCHIPELAGO
Indonesia is the world's largest island group, or archipelago, spreading one-eighth the way around Earth. The western islands lie on a shelf off Southeast Asia, and the southern islands lie on another shelf off Australia. To the north and east, chains of active volcanic islands have been created over plate boundaries.

▼ INDONESIA'S ISLAND POPULATION
Not surprisingly, Indonesia's 235 million people reflect many different tribal groups and are spread out over 6,000 of the 17,000 islands. Today, many Indonesians are moving to find jobs in big cities. Three-quarters of the population now live on 6 main islands, including Sumatra and Java, where overcrowding is becoming a major problem.

BANDANAIRA ISLAND

STEPPING STONES

The islands of Indonesia and the Philippines (the busy island village of Cebu is shown here) provided some of the "stepping stones" used by humans spreading out from Asia across the Pacific Ocean. These voyagers made use of low sea levels to cross between neighbouring islands, reaching Australia at least 60,000 years ago. For millions of years, plants and animals too have island-hopped on the wind and waves. Nowadays, travelling between the islands is relatively easy, as regular ferry services connect the island groups.

islands

◄ GALAPAGOS ISLANDS
The Galapagos are a chain of hot spot volcanic islands off the coast of South America produced from sea-floor eruptions over the last 4 million years. As a result of their isolation, the Galapagos have unique animals and plants, including the marine iguana.

MARINE IGUANA ►
This reptile uses its flat tail to swim in the surf and is the world's only seaweed-eating lizard. English naturalist Charles Darwin visited the Galapagos islands in 1835, and the unique wildlife influenced his theory of evolution.

ALEUTIAN CHAIN, ALASKA
The Aleutians form a volcanic island arc around the northern Pacific Ocean. As the Pacific Plate drifts north into the North American Plate, its front edge sinks into the mantle. Magma rises from the mantle above the sinking plate to form volcanoes, which extend from mid-ocean in the west to the Alaskan coast in the east.

BIRTH OF SURTSEY
Surtsey is one of Earth's youngest islands. It was born in November 1963, when a submarine volcano suddenly erupted off the coast of Iceland. For the next three-and-a-half years, basalt flooded from the seafloor to add to the volcano rising above the waves. Today the little island has an area of about 2.5 km² (1 sq mile).

Corals grow in shallow water fringing volcano

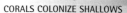

CORALS COLONIZE SHALLOWS

Ring-shaped coral reef grows and encloses peak

REEF APPEARS ABOVE SURFACE

Lagoon forms inside ring of coral as volcano is eroded

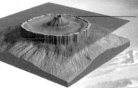

LAGOON COMPLETE

FORMING A CORAL ATOLL
An atoll is a ring-shaped coral reef. It begins to form when skeleton-building corals grow in shallow water around the flanks of an ocean volcano. The corals build the reef up until it rises above the water. The volcano cone is eroded by wave action, and the crater is submerged, leaving just the ring of coral.

Volcanic peak within lagoon

Atoll is colonized by wind-blown or drifting plant seeds

Sandy beach formed from coral limestone

◄ ATOLL ANATOMY
Coral atolls form in the warm shallows of tropical seas, including the Caribbean, the western Pacific, and the Indian Ocean. The living corals are communities of small animals that trap food from the tides. Algae in the coral tissues help them build stony skeletons, which form the ring-shaped reef. Eventually the reef becomes an island, complete with coral sand beaches and colonizing plants and animals. The lagoons, protected from waves, provide calm harbours for shipping.

GLACIERS AND ICE SHEETS

Glaciers are permanent bodies of ice. They form on high mountains in many parts of the world, though the largest glaciers – ice sheets – cover the entire pola region. Glaciers flow slowly downhill, carving deep valleys in rock and calving (shedding) icebergs into the sea where they reach coasts. Today, ice covers one-tenth of Earth's total surface, but at earlier times in Earth's history it has covered an area three times bigger. Though glaciers grow and shrink with changing climates, they leave lasting evidence of their work. Many of o greatest mountain ranges were sculpte by the force of moving ice.

glaciers

HOW A VALLEY GLACIER FORMS

A valley glacier usually starts flowing from a bowl-shaped hollow, known as a cirque. Here, two glaciers from neighbouring cirques are merging into a single flow. Till (rock debris) is heaped up into deposits known as moraines. These deposits are found between the glaciers (medial moraine), at the sides (lateral moraine), and at the end or snout (terminal moraine). At lower altitudes, warmer temperatures melt the ice. The meltwater can form a lake, which is dammed by a wall formed at the end of the glacier.

Cirque: rock basin from which glacier flows

Nunataks: bedrock that projects through the ice

Rock avalanche

Crevasses: deep cracks in the ice

Lateral moraine: rock debris at side

Terminal moraine

Rocks plucked from valley floor

Medial moraine: rock debris trapped between glaciers

Meltwater stream trickles through glacier

Streams

▲ MARGERIE GLACIER, ALASKA

The most common form of glacier is a valley or alpine glacier. It usually flows down a mountain valley originally shaped by a stream. The tongue of moving ice scrapes away rock debris, or till, and bulldozes it into ridges and heaps. In time, the glacier changes the valley into a U-shape. A glacier may flow for just a few hundred metres or for hundreds of kilometres. Looking at a glacier, it is hard to get a sense of scale: these ice cliffs at the tip of the Margerie Glacier rise about 80 m (262 ft) above the water.

MALASPINA GLACIER, ALASKA

Where glaciers spill out of steep valleys into flat areas of land, they form a spreading tongue of ice known as a piedmont lobe. The world's largest piedmont lobe is the Malaspina Glacier, which covers more than 5,000 km² (1,930 sq miles) on the Gulf of Alaska. The outlet from which the glacier spills appears on this satellite image as a neck of ice. The neck looks narrow, but is actually 4 km (2.5 miles) wide. The S-shape to the left is the Agassiz Glacier.

▲ ICE SHEET MARGIN, GREENLAND

Icebergs litter the shores of Greenland. Four-fifths of the island is buried under a giant ice sheet measuring more than 1.7 million km² (656,000 sq miles). The ice sheet is domed, with two high peaks in the interior. Ice flows outwards from the domes to the coast, where the icebergs break away into the North Atlantic. Though vast, the Greenland ice sheet is dwarfed by the Antarctic ice sheet, which is nearly 8 times larger.

◄ ERRATIC BOULDER

As glaciers melt and retreat, they leave behind the rocks they once carried. Some are just pebbles, but others may weigh thousands of tonnes. These rocks are known as erratics. They can often be identified by their rock type, which is older or younger than the supporting rock, which gives scientists vital clues as to how glaciers moved. Glaciers have been known to transport erratics up to 800 km (500 miles).

Firn: compacted snow

Direction of wind

Ice shelf: where ice floats out to sea

Tabular icebergs are flat-topped

▲ HOW AN ICECAP FORMS

An icecap is a small ice sheet. It forms when moisture-laden winds drop snow on mountain slopes. In cold conditions the snow settles year after year. This build-up is called accumulation. As snowflakes are weighed down under new snowfall, they change into ice granules, then into a denser ice known as firn, and, after many years, into hard blue ice. Ice creeps downhill to coasts, where it melts or breaks up into icebergs. This loss of ice is called ablation.

ICEBERGS

Saddle shape formed by wind and wave erosion

Flat-topped berg calved from ice shelf

ARCTIC ICEBERG

Icebergs are floating chunks of freshwater ice that form when glaciers reach the sea. Arctic bergs are much smaller than Antarctic bergs and tend to be more irregular in shape. The oldest icebergs are blue, rather than white; their ice has formed over thousands of years and has had most of the air squeezed out of it.

ANTARCTIC ICEBERG

More than 90% of the world's icebergs are produced from the floating shelves of ice around Antarctica. The shelves are strained by water pressure until table-shaped icebergs calve (break away) into the water. It is a long journey from the glacier to the sea, and the ice in icebergs is an average of 5,000 years old.

ICEBERG SIZE

Only about seven-eighths of an iceberg's volume is visible above the water; the rest is hidden below the surface. Some are huge: in 1956, an iceberg larger than the country of Belgium calved from Antarctica. In 2002, an iceberg 167 m (550 ft) tall was sighted off the coast of Greenland.

SOIL

The top layer of Earth's surface is made up of rock particles, minerals, air, water, and organic matter. Soil is produced when bedrock – the solid rock that lies under these particles – is weathered into tiny pieces and chemically altered by rainwater. The rate of weathering depends on rock type and climate, and there are many different kinds of soil. Soil's organic content, humus, comes from the plants, animals, and bacteria living within it. Soil is a life-support system. Plants depend on it, and we need it for growing food. But where humans do not manage soil carefully, it is quickly eroded or used up. It takes centuries to produce, and is not easily replaced.

Plants: take in nutrients from humus

Humus: organic material, made up of decayed plant and animal matter

Topsoil: rich in humus and life-forms, such as earthworms

Subsoil: poor in humus, rich in minerals washed down from above

Weathered rock: high content of minerals from fragments of parent rock

Bedrock: unweathered parent rock, from which soil is ultimately formed

◄ SOIL LAYERS
As soil forms, it settles into layers. Scientists class the layers in bands known as horizons, and together they make up a soil profile, which varies from one place to another. In this diagram of a mature forest soil, the upper horizons make up the topsoil, rich in humus, or organic matter. The subsoil below collects minerals washed out of the topsoil. At the very bottom lies the parent rock: the bedrock from which the soil is created by weathering.

▲ SOIL ENRICHERS
By burrowing through the ground and feeding on humus, earthworms help aerate the soil and mix up the mineral and organic content. In tropical grasslands, ground-dwelling termites play a similar role of transporting nutrients to the topsoil. Other soil enrichers include fungi and bacteria. They speed up the decay of plant and animal remains, turning them into humus, which is food for other organisms, such as trees.

▲ INTENSIVE FARMING
All our major food crops are grown in soil. As the world's population rises, the supply of good farming soil is running low. Crops take nutrients, such as nitrogen, out of soil, and farmers replace these by applying fertilizers. Meanwhile, agronomists - soil scientists - research ways of improving soil fertility, irrigation (watering), and drainage. They also look into producing new strains of higher-yielding crops that can produce more food from the same area.

FOREST SOIL

...orested regions with a mild, moist climate, rainwater flushes ...s and oxides from the topsoil. They build up in the subsoil, ...ch is a rich red-brown colour. Abundant forest vegetation adds ...he humus content of the topsoil, which is highly acidic and pale. ...kind of soil, called pedalfer, is common across the eastern ...ted States and much of Europe. It makes good farmland.

**FOREST SOIL
CLOSE-UP**

TROPICAL SOIL

...pical warmth and high rainfall lead to quick weathering and a ...ep soil layer. However, plant growth is also rapid, and nutrients ...end little time in the topsoil. Minerals like silica and calcium ...rbonate are washed away, leaving a bright orange-red topsoil ...at is high in oxides and clay. Known as laterite, this soil can be ...rmed for only a year or two before it is exhausted.

**TROPICAL SOIL
CLOSE-UP**

▲ SOIL EROSION IN GAIZI VALLEY, CHINA

This valley in China has lost its soil through erosion. When soil is used repeatedly for growing crops, without a break between sowings, it becomes unstable. The removal of plant cover leaves it at the mercy of the wind and rain, which remove the soil and dump it in rivers. Across about one-third of the world's croplands, soil is being eroded faster than it is being replaced. The United States, for example, loses about 2 billion tonnes (2.2 billion tons) of topsoil each year.

▲ DESERT SOIL

Just as soil production speeds up under tropical conditions, it practically grinds to a halt in the parched ground of desert and dry scrubland. The topsoil is stony, and its mineral content is much like that of the parent rock below. Water tends to dry off before it has the chance to sink in, and the subsoil contains a chalky layer of calcium carbonate left behind by the process of evaporation.

**DESERT SOIL
CLOSE-UP**

PROPERTIES OF CLAY

This clay-based soil has dried out and diminished in volume, creating cracks in the surface. Clay is made up of very fine mineral particles. It is an important ingredient in soil, storing up gases and minerals that are necessary for plant growth. However, too much clay in soil reduces its ability to soak up and store valuable water. Some clays swell when water is added to them, and shrink when dry. Others are non-expanding: they simply go soft when water is added. These are the clays used, for example, in the ceramics industry.

◄ SHANGHAI
Shanghai is China's key
transport centre and one o
the world's biggest seaport
The Huangpu River flows
through its centre before
entering the Yangtze River
nearby. At high tide, cargo
ships can sail upriver from
ocean right into the city. Th
world's first cities grew up
the banks of rivers such as
Indus, Tigris, and Euphrates,
where people depended on
water to irrigate their crops

The Huangpu River is
113 km (70 miles) long

RIVERS

Rivers play a role in the water cycle by collecting rainfall
that runs off the land and carrying it back to the oceans.
On the way, they irrigate the land, supporting different
ecosystems. Rivers leave their mark on the land, eroding
rock and soil and carving deep valleys. When they reach
the oceans, they deposit minerals and nutrients that help
support marine life. Rivers provide various
other benefits, from shipping lanes to fresh
water, and their banks have been home to
the world's greatest cities. But they also
create danger in the form of floods.

rivers

Watershed
separating
drainage basins

Tributaries join
the main stream

Drainage basin
extends either side
of river

ANATOMY OF A RIVER
A river collects runoff – rain or snow that runs off the land
into rivers or seas rather than soaking in or evaporating –
and transfers it back to the oceans. Along the length of the
river valley, streams known as tributaries drain into the river.

WORLD'S LONGEST RIVERS

▲ YANGTZE
Flowing for 6,300 km (3,912 miles) through
Tibet and China, the Yangtze is the largest river
in Asia and the third largest in the world. Its
source lies about 5,500 m (18,040 ft) above sea
level in the Plateau of Tibet, and the river winds
through deep valleys for much of its length.

▲ NILE
The Nile is the world's longest river. It starts in
the mountains of East Africa and flows into
Lake Victoria, before winding north through
Sudan and Egypt to the Mediterranean on its
6,650-km (4,130-mile) journey. Heavy rains in
Ethiopia cause the Nile to flood every summer.

▲ AMAZON
The Amazon is the world's second-longest river,
flowing nearly 6,400 km (4,100 miles) across
equatorial South America to the Atlantic Ocean.
The river follows a winding course through the
flat, low-lying Amazon rainforest. It floods
every year, drowning the forest for months.

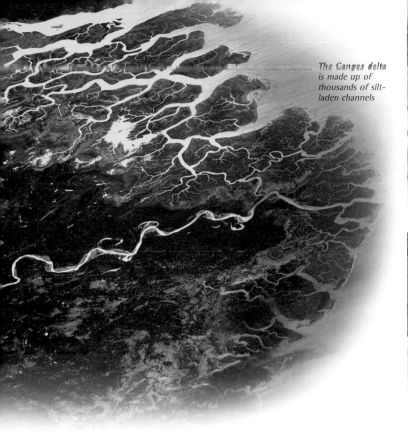

The Ganges delta is made up of thousands of silt-laden channels

FERTILE FARMLAND, NILE VALLEY ▲
Thousands of years ago, the Ancient Egyptian civilization flourished on the banks of the Nile. The river's annual flood deposited rich silt on the floodplains, creating a slim corridor of fertile land in the desert. Since 1970 the Aswan High Dam has controlled the floodwaters to make farming easier in the dry season. However, the dam stops the river from depositing silt, so farmers now have to use fertilizers to make their crops grow.

NGES DELTA
anges River starts in the Himalayas and winds across India and adesh for 2,510 km (1,560 miles). It is joined in Bangladesh by the naputra River, and they empty into the Bay of Bengal. Entering ay, the current slows, and the water deposits sediment. Years of ition have formed a vast, flat tongue of sediment known as a over which the river splits into many separate streams.

ES OF RIVER

◄ THREE GORGES DAM, CHINA
China's Yangtze River floods regularly, killing thousands of people each year. In 1992 the Chinese government began building a dam across it. The Three Gorges Dam is due to be finished by 2009. It is intended to control the flooding, and also to provide a clean source of electricity.

SEASONAL, CRETE
The Mallia River on the Greek island of Crete is swollen by springtime rain. Crete's rivers are especially short and flow over rocky hillsides. There is very little annual runoff to keep them flowing all year. In regions with a Mediterranean climate, rivers may dry up entirely during the long, hot summers.

EPHEMERAL, AUSTRALIA

A pool shrinking under the desert sun is all that remains of the Todd River in Australia's hot Northern Territory. It is a so-called ephemeral river – one that flows only occasionally. Once every year or so, brief and heavy rains cause the Todd to burst its banks, but the water soon evaporates or soaks into the ground.

PERENNIAL, USA

Giant rivers like the Mississippi never stop. "Old Man River" flows 3,780 km (2,347 miles) from Lake Itasca, Minnesota, through the USA to the Gulf of Mexico. It is the longest river in North America, draining an area of 4.76 million km² (1.83 million sq miles) that includes 31 US states and 2 Canadian provinces.

▲ FLOODING IN BANGLADESH
Bangladesh lies on the delta of several large rivers, including the Ganges, Meghna, Surma, and Jamuna. The countryside is flat and low-lying, and the rivers shift their course every year. Devastating floods happen regularly, sweeping away animals and people. But the floods are not entirely unwelcome, since they bring rich silt that improves the soil and helps crops grow.

CAVES

Caves are spectacular natural spaces created out of rock by the action of water. For instance, the lapping of waves against a cliff can gradually erode (wear away) the rock face to create a cave. Caves also form when buried rock, usually limestone, is dissolved by groundwater – rainwater that has soaked into the land. Other rocks, such as sandstone, slowly collect groundwater like a sponge and store it. Groundwater is a precious freshwater resource. It feeds rivers and lakes during dry seasons, and supplies many homes, farms, and industries.

CAVE BATS ►
Caves offer bats a habitat for breeding and resting in large groups called colonies. In the tropics, bat colonies spend the day in a cave before flying out at dusk to hunt flying insects or feed on tree fruits. (By hunting at night, they avoid competing with birds for the same food resources.) In cooler regions, bats find less to eat as winter approaches, and many species find the stable temperature of a cave ideal for their long winter sleep.

HOW A STALACTITE FORMS ►
Groundwater is mildly acidic because it contains carbon dioxide captured from the air. As it flows through a layer of limestone, the acid dissolves calcite from it, creating the spaces that become caves. But when water drips from a cave ceiling, some of the water evaporates to the air. This makes the water release a tiny trace of calcite on the ceiling. Drip by drip, trace by trace, the calcite deposits build up into a stalactite.

Calcite deposits from dripping water form main body of stalactite

Drop of water at tip of stalactite

▲ CAVE PAINTINGS
Our prehistoric ancestors knew all about the caves in their territories, and made full use of them for shelter and defence from other humans and predatory animals. The earliest known art is in the form of paintings on the walls of caves. These beautiful bison-like creatures are copies of originals found in the caves at Lascaux, in southern France. These animals were obviously important to our ancestors, and were painted with great care.

◄ STALACTITES AND CAVE INTERIOR
Calcite deposits can turn a cave interior into a fantastical
landscape. When calcium-rich water drips from stalactites, it leaves
a trace of calcite on the floor directly below. These traces slowly
build up into a mound called a stalagmite. A stalagmite may grow
so tall that it merges with the stalactite above to form a complete
column in an underground cave. It takes hundreds or even
thousands of years to form large stalactites
and stalagmites.

caves

Sinkhole allows water underground

Chimney is a near-vertical opening in rock

Gallery is a large underground chamber

Stalactite hangs down from the roof of the cave

Stalagmite rises from the floor of the cave

Impermeable layer through which water cannot pass

Underground lake

▲ CAVE CHARACTERISTICS
Limestone caves form during periods when the rock mass is soaked through with groundwater.
Weakly acidic water flows into pockets and cracks in the rock, dissolving away calcite from roofs,
walls, and floors alike. Horizontal cracks open out into flooded gallery caves linked together in complex
systems. In time, the surrounding landscape changes. Rivers drain the caves, finding exits above deep layers
of harder rock. But groundwater continues to filter through the caves, forming stalactites and stalagmites.

▲ UNDERWATER SPRINGS
An oasis survives in the desert, thanks to the water table. Below a
certain depth, groundwater fills every available pore in rock or soil.
The upper limit of this waterlogged zone is called the water table.
Above that, there is a mixture of air and water. In a valley or a
desert basin where the water table is near or even above the
surface, groundwater is available as a spring, a well, or a lake.

▲ SINKHOLE COLLAPSE
When water creates limestone caves close to the ground surface, the cave roof
may become so thin that it collapses without warning, forming a sinkhole. This
huge hole opened up in a city car park in Atlanta, Georgia, USA in 1993; other
sinkholes have been known to swallow whole houses. Regions that are heavily
pitted with sinkholes are called karst landscapes. They are named after the Karst
region of Slovenia in eastern Europe, where such terrain is common.

DESERTS

There are many different kinds of deserts. Those that are hot all year are called hot deserts. They lie within 15-35 degrees north or south of the equator. Cold deserts are found farther north or south. They may be hot in summer, but are cold and dry in winter. Rain-shadow deserts are dry because nearby mountains stop moist air from bringing rain to them. West coast deserts, swept by cold dry ocean winds, are some of the driest places on Earth. All deserts have one feature in common: an annual rainfall of less than 400 mm (16 in).

◄ SAHARA
The Sahara is a hot desert, and one of the world's largest at 9 million km² (3.5 million sq miles). It is a landscape of rocky plains, basins, and plateaus, as well as sand seas. Today the Sahara is hot and dusty, but its climate used to be milder and moister. Fossils show that it was once a fertile land with rivers and lakes.

DESERTS		3.7% EARTH'S SURFACE

TYPE	AREA	PRINCIPAL LOCATIONS
Hot desert	77%	N Africa, Arabia, India
Cold desert	18%	C Asia
Rain-shadow	3.5%	Chile, California
West coast	1.5%	Namibia, Peru

Telson, or stinger, contains venom

Pedipalps are powerful pincers

◄ SCORPION
Scorpions are arachnids, relatives of spiders and mites. They survive in the desert by avoiding the daytime Sun. Some species hide under rocks, while others lurk in sandy burrows that they dig with their 8 legs. At night they come out to hunt for insects, lizards, and rodents. The cuticle, or outer skeleton, has a waxy coating that helps keep body fluids from drying out.

◄ CAMEL
Dromedary camels (with a single hump) are native to Arabia, but have been used in northern Africa since the days of Ancient Egypt. They helped traders ferry ivory, salt, and gold across the Sahara, and carried native tribes into desert battles. They can travel for up to two weeks without needing to drink, and, unlike sheep and cattle, they do not overgraze desert plants.

DESERT PLANTLIFE

STURT'S DESERT PEA
This plant is a flowering herb that grows in the deserts of central and southern Australia. The grey leaves are coated in fine, short hairs that trap water and keep the leaf surfaces damp. The seeds have a hard coating that protects them through long droughts, but when rain falls they rapidly sprout long roots.

PALM TREES
Desert peoples of Africa and Asia have grown the date palm for thousands of years, putting it to hundreds of uses. For example, they get food from its fruit, flowers, and pollen; alcohol from its sap; rope from the leaf fibres; timber from the trunk; and charcoal from the date stones. The tree grows near oases, not in the desert.

CACTI
Superbly adapted to life in the American deserts, cacti grow in all shapes and sizes. The juicy stems swell up during rainy periods to hold water reserves for the dry months. Most cacti have spines in place of leaves (which would lose too much water). Spines also prevent animals from nibbling the stems and damaging them.

TAMARISK
These trees grow up to 3 m (10 ft) tall and thrive in the deserts of central Asia, even in very salty soils. The long roots tap into stored water deep below the ground, so the trees do not depend on rainfall. In long droughts, tamarisks simply shed the scale-like leaves on their slender branches and become inactive.

◄ DESERT RECLAMATION
Anything will grow in a desert if you use enough water. In these circular fields in New Mexico, USA, pipes take water from deep beneath the desert's surface or from the Colorado River, and sprinkle it over crops. But careless irrigation can be destructive. It may pollute rivers and poison desert plants with salty minerals.

ATACAMA DESERT ►
The Atacama Desert on the west coast of South America is both a rain-shadow desert and a west coast desert. The mountain ranges of the Andes to the east force moist air to shed its rain before reaching it. Any ocean winds that do reach the desert from the west contain little moisture because they blow in over cold water. The Atacama has large deposits of salt, which accumulate in basins called salars.

deserts

Plateau: a large flat area with steep cliffs

Wadi: a dry gully eroded by flash floods

Mesa: a small, separate plateau

DESERT FEATURES ►
Loose sand is heaped into straight, curving, or pyramidal dunes by the wind. Water erodes rocky hills to create flat tables. Torrents from brief rainfall carve gullies in rock and spread fans of sediment in low basins. Water either evaporates from basins or soaks away. Oases are islands of life that form in low-lying areas where water is found at or near the surface.

Inselberg: an island of erosion-resistant rock

Crescent dunes formed by wind

Wind direction affects shape of dune formation

Oasis: water source that supports plantlife

TROPICAL FORESTS

Tropical forests are found in lands on or near the equator, where the Sun's heat is at its greatest, and warm, rising air drops heavy rainfall. There are many kinds of tropical forests. Some are hot, with long, dry seasons. Others are cloaked in cool mist on high mountains. The best known are the lowland rainforests, which are permanently warm and wet. Although tropical forest covers less than three per cent of the Earth's surface, it harbours more plant and animal life than any other biome on Earth.

TROPICAL FORESTS		2.8% EARTH'S SURFACE

TYPE	AREA	PRINCIPAL LOCATIONS
Wet forests	82%	S America, SE Asia, C Africa
Dry forests	18%	India, C America, Africa

◄ DRY FOREST
In a monsoon forest, warm summer winds blow in off the ocean, bringing heavy rain. Cool, dry winds blow the other way during winter, creating a dry season. A monsoon forest has a lower, more open canopy than a rainforest, allowing light to reach the floor, which becomes thick and jungle-like.

tropical forests

WET FOREST ►
In a lowland rainforest, thousands of plant species live jumbled together and tend to form several layers. The treetop "canopy" takes most of the light, and the layers grow steadily darker, cooler, and damper towards the shady forest floor. Leaves are large, waxy, and thick, with "drip tips" – drooping, pointed ends that shed water easily to avoid unhealthy waterlogging.

▲ EVERGREEN HOLLY
While some of the upper-canopy trees in a monsoon forest shed their leaves during the dry season, trees and shrubs such as holly, in the lower layers, usually keep their foliage. This makes these forests semi-evergreen.

FLOODED FORESTS OF THE AMAZON

Tropical forests become flooded when rivers burst their banks after high rainfall. In parts of the Amazon, trees spend up to 7 months of the year standing in water that may be tens of metres deep. Buttress roots act like props around the base of the trunk to help stop them falling. The deep waterways of the Amazon are home to a freshwater dolphin, known locally as the boto. It has a long slim beak, which it uses to probe for food in the mud on the riverbed. It feeds on crabs, river turtles, and catfish.

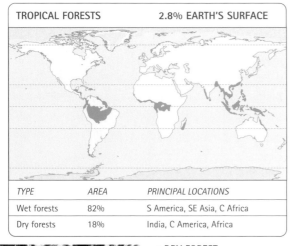

...RGENT

...allest rainforest trees have ...ht trunks with branches only ...e crown (top). These giant ... are known as "emergents" ...use their crowns "emerge" ... the canopy into full light.

Toucan bill
is hollow with sharp,
saw-like edges for
holding fruit

TOCO TOUCAN ▶
The toucan is at home in the
rainforest, where it nests in tree holes
and uses its huge bill to crush and
chop fruits. While flying, the toucan often
drops fruits to the floor. Many of these grow
into new trees, increasing the toucan's food supply.

...NOPY

...eights of 20–30 m (66–98 ft), ...crowns of tall trees spread out ...l they almost touch, fitting ...ether like a jigsaw, forming ...almost unbroken leafy canopy ...t traps most of the sunlight.

◀ SQUIRREL MONKEY
At home in the high canopy of Central
and South American rainforests,
squirrel monkeys live in large groups,
numbering 50 or more. They feed on
anything from fruit to spiders and
young birds in nests.

BROMELIAD ▶
Bromeliads are epiphytes – plants that
are not rooted in the soil but which
grow perched on tree branches. Their
roots take up moisture and nutrients
from the tree or from the air itself.

Long leaves
collect rainwater

...NDERSTOREY

...naller trees often form a lower ...nopy about 15 m (49 ft) above ...e ground, filtering out much of ...e light, so that in some forests ...ly 2–3% of the available light ...aches the forest floor.

◀ SPINY DEVIL KATYDID
Katydids are some of the noisiest rainforest insects.
The males rasp their wings together to "sing" loudly for
a mate. Many katydids eat flowers and leaves, though
some attack tiny insects trapped in water pools in
plants. In turn, katydids are prey for birds, bats, and
monkeys. They tend to be green
and leaf-shaped, and
perch motionless to
avoid being eaten.

Large eyes
help to spot prey and
judge attack distances

Spines on the body
discourage birds or
monkeys from making the
katydid their next meal

...FOREST FLOOR

...he dark forest floor consists of ...tree roots covered in leaf litter, ...which is recycled by billions of ants ...and termites. Fungi in the soil also ...convert the debris into nutrients, ...which are absorbed by the roots.

Leaves form pitchers (jugs)
that attract flies and other
insects by exuding a
strong-smelling nectar

GABOON VIPER ▶
Snakes rely on the Sun's
heat to warm their bodies,
so they thrive in tropical
forests. This Gaboon viper
lives on the African
rainforest floor. It has
the longest fangs of
any snake, measuring
up to 50 mm (2 in).

Skin pattern
acts as camouflage on
the forest floor

PITCHER PLANT ▶
Where rainforest soils
are poor, plants find
nutrients in unusual
ways. A pitcher plant
traps and digests
insects inside its
fluid-filled pitcher.

TEMPERATE FORESTS

Temperate forests grow where temperature, rainfall, and hours of sunlight change a lot through the year. The boreal, or coniferous, forest is a vast belt around the northern hemisphere, made up of evergreen, cone-bearing trees. Broadleaf deciduous forests flourish in cool, wet winters and mild, moist summers. These trees, which include oak and beech, shed their leaves in winter to conserve energy. Mediterranean forests are characterised by the dry summers and mild winters typical of the Mediterranean. Temperate rainforest often grows beside mountains on mild, rainy coasts.

TEMPERATE FORESTS		4.7% EARTH'S SURFACE
TYPE	*AREA*	*PRINCIPAL LOCATIONS*
Deciduous	56%	Canada, Siberia
Coniferous	32%	Tasmania, W Europe
Mediterranean	11%	Mediterranean, California
Rainforest	1%	NW USA, Chile, NZ, Japan

temperate forests

▲ BROWN BEAR
The long temperate winters drive many mammals into hibernation. This is a deep sleep in which the heartbeat slows down and the body uses very little energy. The brown bear hibernates for up to 7 months each year in a den among tree roots or in a cave. It does not wake to feed, but survives on body fat stored up in autumn. The female even gives birth in her den.

▲ CONIFEROUS PINES IN SNOW
Cone-bearing trees, known as conifers, are most common in cool, temperate zones and on mountain slopes, where their short branches help them to shed snow and rain easily. The densely growing boreal forests contain just a few, very hardy conifer species. Their leaves are needle-shaped and have a waxy surface, so that they lose little water. Since they remain on the tree all year round, the needles start soaking up the Sun's warmth as early as possible in spring. Their dark colour also helps them absorb sunlight.

▲ DOUGLAS FIR CONE
These are cones of the Douglas fir, native to western North America. A conifer produces two kinds of cone on the same tree: male cones, which bear pollen, and female cones, which contain eggs. Blown by the wind, some of the pollen reaches the female cones and fertilizes the eggs, which produce seeds. After ripening, the seeds scatter, falling to the ground and becoming embedded in the soil to produce new growth.

▲ GREY WOLF
The grey wolf was once widespread in North America, Europe, and Asia. Fear of this predator drove settlers to destroy all but a few wolf packs, which lived deep in the northern forests, mountains, and tundra. Today these habitats are the wolf's stronghold. Wolves live in packs. Hunting together, they bring down animals as large as deer and moose, then share the kill.

REST FIRES

or millions of years, fire has played a role in the ecology of forests. It changes the mix of plant and imal species, and returns nutrients such as nitrogen to the soil. Some trees, such as the Douglas fir, row thick bark as they mature, which helps them survive fire. Today, human activities are disturbing atural burning patterns, sometimes leading to uncontrollable fires that can destroy forests.

▲ DECIDUOUS FOREST
Each year, the onset of cold autumn weather and the drop in light levels cause deciduous trees to shed their leaves. Fresh leaves grow in spring to continue the role of photosynthesis – using the Sun's energy to turn carbon dioxide and water into sugars for food. Meanwhile, fallen leaves create a carpet of decaying organic matter that nourishes plants, fungi, and insects such as beetles. Open deciduous woodlands contain a floor cover of shrubs such as hazel.

▲ CROCUSES
A crocus times its flowering to make the most of changing conditions in deciduous woodland. In winter and summer it stores food in its corm, an underground bulb-like structure. It typically flowers in early spring, when the temperature rises but tree branches are still bare, letting the Sun's rays through to warm the forest floor. Some crocuses flower in autumn, after the trees have shed their leaves.

▲ TEMPERATE RAINFOREST
On certain shores, moist winds from the ocean shed heavy rain on coastal forests. A mild climate, high humidity, and heavy rainfall make ideal growth conditions for some of the world's largest trees, such as the 100-m (328-ft) high redwoods of the American Pacific Northwest.

▲ FERNS
Temperate rainforests are thick with climbers, moss, and understorey plants. Ferns thrive in warm, wet forests. Their leaves first appear as croziers – shoots shaped like a shepherd's crook that gradually unfurl. The leaves shed tiny cells called spores, which produce new plants.

GRASSLANDS

Before it was reduced by the spread of crop farming and ranching, grassland covered as much as two-fifths of Earth's land surface. It is found from the cold northern plains to the hot tropics, and takes many forms, which all share certain features. For example, the annual rainfall usually lies between 250 and 800 mm (10–31 in). This is too low for trees to take root, too high for desert to take over, but ideal for non-woody, flowering plants such as grasses. Many grasses grow best if they are regularly burned.

GRASSLANDS		6% EARTH'S SURFACE
TYPE	*AREA*	*PRINCIPAL LOCATIONS*
Temperate	67%	Australia, Russia, China, N America
Tropical	33%	Sub-Saharan Africa, Brazil, Mexico

▼ SERENGETI SAVANNA
In the Serengeti National Park in Tanzania, East Africa, mammals graze the lightly wooded, tropical grassland known as savanna. The largest, such as the elephant and buffalo, graze and trample the longest grasses, making way for wildebeest and zebra, which graze shorter grasses. Tiny, delicate gazelles graze the short stems. The grazers migrate from one waterhole to another as the seasons change, followed by big cats and other predators.

LIFE IN THE TROPICAL GRASSLANDS

TERMITE MOUND
Termites are insects that live in colonies. Many tropical grassland species build soil mounds, an activity that brings nutrients up to the surface vegetation. Termites eat dung, grass, and organic particles in soil, and are among the few animals that can digest cellulose (a tough substance in plant cells).

SABLE ANTELOPE
Feeding out in the open is dangerous: grazers must keep watch for hyenas, lions, and leopards. Hoofed mammals of the savanna have evolved lean, light limbs for fleeing fast, and some - like the sable antelope - have sharp horns, too, to defend themselves as a last resort if there is nowhere left to run.

grasslands

CHEETAH ▶
The cheetah is the world's fastest land animal, sprinting at up to 110 kph (68 mph) in short bursts while chasing small antelope prey. This makes it unlike any other large African predator. But although special skills bring advantages, they also create problems. The cheetah has evolved into such an open-grassland expert that it cannot hunt in any other habitat type. And as grassland disappears under the plough, the cheetah has become rare.

NORTH AMERICAN PRAIRIE

Temperate grassland in North America is called prairie. Varying climate conditions across the continent create three prairie types: tallgrass in the east, mixed-grass on the Great Plains, and shortgrass to the drier west and south. In the past, fires (some started by lightning, others deliberately by Native Americans) burned off dry grasses each year, promoting fresh growth. Around 79% of the original prairie has been built on or converted to farmland.

LIFE IN THE TEMPERATE GRASSLANDS

WHEAT
More than half a billion tonnes of wheat are grown in the world each year, and Canada and the United States are among the top 6 producing countries. The crop is grown upon former prairie lands, where the soil is now so exhausted that farmers have to fertilize it heavily every year in order to reap a satisfactory harvest.

PRAIRIE DOGS
These plump, burrowing rodents of the plains grow up to 30 cm (12 in) long, and live in large warrens known as towns. The towns have sleeping chambers, food stores, and emergency exits for escape from their main predators, which are ferrets or snakes. Their name comes from their habit of giving a sharp, repeated bark to warn one another of danger.

ENDANGERED BISON ▶
The plains bison is a wild American relative of domestic cattle. The powerful bulls weigh up to a tonne. Bison herds once ranged across North America in their tens of millions, but during the 1800s white settlers slaughtered the animals for their hides and meat. Bison were also killed in order to starve the Plains Indians, and by the 1880s were nearly extinct. Today, after more than a century of protection, their future is secure.

DUSTBOWL IN AMERICAN MIDWEST ▶
High winds on the Great Plains between 1935 and 1938 blew away so much soil that a vast area of 40 million km² (15.6 million sq miles) was left a wasteland. Americans called it the Dustbowl. The damage had started in the 1860s, when settlers grew the wrong kind of wheat and allowed cattle to overgraze the plains. Root systems were gradually destroyed, so that the soil was easily stripped away when the storms struck.

Clouds of dust blotted out the Sun and swamped farms during the storms of the 1930s

WETLANDS

Wetlands include any site where the soil is waterlogged part or all of the time. They comprise fresh and saltwater habitats, from bogs and swamps to coastal mangrove forests. Wetlands are vital refuges for animals, help cleanse polluted waterways, and buffer the land against extreme weather, acting like a big sponge to control floods. But their dependence on water makes them fragile, and because their importance is often ignored, wetlands are today some of the most threatened of all the Earth's biomes.

WETLANDS	2.5% EARTH'S SURFACE	
TYPE	AREA	PRINCIPAL LOCATIONS (EXAMPLE)
Inland	67%	Worldwide (Okavango Delta)
Coastal	21%	Worldwide (Amazon)
River	12%	Worldwide (Gulf of Mexico)

Wings are capable of carrying them great distances

DRAGONFLY ▲
Dragonflies are fierce hunters with superb vision. They are found near wetlands because they depend on water for part of their life cycle. The nymph (larva) spends up to 5 years underwater.

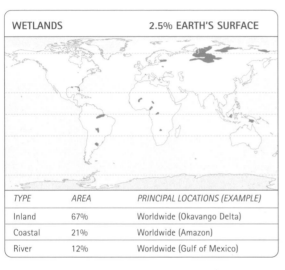

▲ RIVER
Rivers are continually changing. For example, silt carried in the water erodes the banks in places where the current is strong, but is deposited in slow-flowing sections to form banks. Together, erosion and deposition alter a river's course. Heavy flooding creates temporary wetlands on the floodplains. These nourish the soil and also attract flocks of migrant birds.

▲ GREY HERON
The grey heron is one of the top predators in the food web of a European river. (It is replaced in North America by the great blue heron.) The heron hunts fish and frogs, sometimes by standing in wait, but also by stalking through shallows, its neck hunched in readiness to strike with its long, stabbing bill. Other top river predators include the otter, mink, and, in slow rivers, pike.

▲ INLAND WETLAND, NORTH CAROLINA
In North America, bald cypress and water tupelo are two trees adapted to standing in water for part or all of the year. They survive swamp life by sending out "knees" – gnarled stilt-like support roots around the base of the trunk. The knees are thought to stabilize the tree and also to take up oxygen. Animals of the swamps include wood duck, egrets, and black bears.

THE ARAL SEA

The Aral Sea, located in Uzbekistan and Kazakhstan, was once the world's fourth largest inland sea, with an area the size of Southern California. About 40 years ago, its level started dropping, when vast amounts of water were diverted for cotton irrigation to satisfy Soviet agricultural production requirements. The sea has shrunk so much that its surface area has more than halved, its volume has decreased by 75%, and parts of the sea-bed have become salty desert. If present trends continue, the Aral Sea will disappear altogether.

wetlands

ALLIGATOR ►

The American alligator plays an important role in wetland ecosystems of the southeastern United States. To survive the dry season, when it is inactive, an alligator digs itself a watery hole in the mud. Other wetland creatures, from frogs and fish to turtles, hide in these "gator holes" until the rains return to swell their usual habitat.

High-set eyes and nostrils allow alligator to see and breathe while submerged

Hinged, bony plates strengthen the scales and provide protection

▲ MOSQUITO
Like the dragonfly, the mosquito spends the larval stage of its life cycle in stagnant water. To nourish the eggs in her abdomen before laying them, the female stabs the skin of another animal, such as a frog, a bird, or a mammal, and draws off a meal of blood. Some mosquito species spread a dangerous disease called malaria, which is the world's number one natural killer.

▲ COASTAL WETLAND, FLORIDA EVERGLADES
The Everglades lies in subtropical Florida, USA. At its heart lies a vast peatland, created by the slow build-up of dead plants. After rain, fresh water drifts south through a mosaic of grassy marshes and "hammocks" (tree islands), which give way farther south to coastal salt marshes and mangrove swamps. The region is threatened today by drainage for agriculture and domestic use.

▲ MANATEE
The West Indian manatee is an aquatic mammal that feeds on water plants. Swimming with the use of broad flippers and a spade-like tail, it cruises the mangrove swamps and rivers of the Gulf of Mexico, grazing heavily on sea grasses and other water plants. Feeding for up to 8 hours daily, the manatee helps keep coastal wetlands free of choking water weeds.

THE ARCTIC

Fringing the top of the northern continents lies
a vast, treeless plain dotted with lakes: the Arctic
tundra. The Arctic region receives little sunlight.
Winters are long and dark, with little snowfall, and the
soil is deep-frozen all year. Plants need to be tough
and low-growing, and they include mosses and lichens.
North of the tundra lies the Arctic Ocean. The waters
surrounding the North Pole are covered with sea ice,
which spreads and retreats with the changing seasons.
Though the climate is hostile, the Arctic region is rich
in insect, mammal, fish, and bird life.

polar regions

◄ THE ARCTIC
The Arctic biome effectively starts north of the
treeline – the line beyond which trees cannot grow.
It is defined by the Arctic Circle at latitude 66' 30"
North. The Arctic Ocean, at 14 million km² (5.5 million
sq miles), is the world's smallest ocean. It contains the
geographic North Pole, which lies under shifting sea ice.
Surrounding the ocean are the northern limits of North
America and Eurasia. Greenland lies mostly within the
Arctic Circle and is permanently iced over.

▲ POLAR BEAR ON SEA ICE
A powerful swimmer, the polar bear hunts seals among the
broken sea ice, relying on creamy-yellow fur for camouflage
and thick body fat for warmth. It also hunts seals on land,
running at speeds up to 55 kph (34 mph), and digs seal pups
from their dens in the snow. The bear needs about 2 kg (4½ lb)
of fat in its diet per day, and when seals are scarce it eats
anything from birds' eggs and fish to seaweed. In the winter,
it saves energy by resting in a den. The pregnant female gives
birth to two cubs between November and January.

ANTARCTICA

Antarctica is an icebound continent surrounding the
South Pole. The ice forms glaciers that shed mighty
icebergs into the Southern Ocean. Like the Arctic,
Antarctica receives little sunlight: the Sun does not rise
at all between late March and September. Even in
summer, 85 per cent of the Sun's heat is reflected by the
ice. So little snow falls each year that the mainland is
effectively a cold desert where few animals can survive.
But the waters are rich in nutrients, and
both the ocean and its remote island
groups teem with wildlife.

polar regions

▲ WEATHER STATION
In the early 1900s, explorers battled the
intense cold to reach the South Pole. Since
the 1950s, Antarctica has been a centre for
international scientific research. Geologists
drill deep into the ice to collect samples laid
down thousands of years ago, and use them
to measure changes in the world's climate.
Fossils show that millions of years ago – before
it drifted south and froze – Antarctica was a
warm land where trees and reptiles once lived.

◄ ANTARCTICA
Beyond the mainland, the Antarctic includes the Southern
Ocean and several islands, such as the Kerguelen, Crozet,
South Shetland, and South Orkney groups. The mainland is
notched with the Weddell and Ross Seas, and the Antarctic
Peninsula threads between them. Sea ice surrounds
Antarctica all year, covering 4 million km² (1.6 million sq miles)
in summer and 5 times that area in winter.

◄ MAKING AN IGLOO

Humans have lived in the Arctic for thousands of years. They include the Aleut, Inuit, Yupiit, Yakut, and Sami people. The various races range right around the far north, from Alaska, Canada, and Greenland east to Siberia. Traditional families live in an igloo like this or a stone hut. They eat fish, whale, seal, and walrus meat, using other body parts for tools, clothing, and shelters. But today, many communities live modern lifestyles.

Thick skin is flushed pink with blood when on land

Bristles up to 30 cm (12 in) long help the walrus forage on murky sea-beds

WALRUS ►

The walrus is a mammal found in shallow Arctic seas. It gathers in great crowds on sea ice or rocky beaches, where males use their tusks to fight with each other over mates. Awkward on land, the walrus swims powerfully. Thick skin keeps it warm when diving to the sea-bed for clams and mussels, which it finds with stiff bristles on its snout. In spring, the female comes to the beach to give birth to a single calf, which she nurses for about 2 years.

EMPEROR PENGUIN ►

The emperor is the only penguin that breeds solely on the Antarctic mainland. It is an incredible feat. The female lays her egg in May. As she returns to the sea to feed, the male tucks the egg in a pouch under his belly and incubates it through the winter. He huddles with other males for warmth and lives off stored body fat. In July, the fluffy coated chick hatches, and the female finally returns to relieve her starving mate.

Dense, fur-like coat of short feathers keeps water out

◄ HUMPBACK WHALE

Humpbacks visit Antarctica during summer to feast on fish and swarms of krill – small, shrimp-like crustaceans that feed on plant and animal plankton. Humpback whales are recognizable by having the longest flippers of any animal, with knobbly leading edges. They are extremely vocal, and the male can produce a long, complex series of sounds. Other migrant whales include the blue, pygmy blue, sei, fin, southern right, and minke.

MARINE

The oceans, which make up Earth's largest biome, can be divided into three zones: inshore water, continental margin, and open sea. Oceans are also zoned by depth. The top 200 m (660 ft) is the sunlit zone, where conditions vary greatly. Below it, in the mesopelagic zone, conditions are more stable. The bathypelagic zone, or deep ocean, is a dark and little-studied world of life-forms with extraordinary adaptations.

marine

SQUID ▶
The squid feeds on shrimp and small fish in the open seas. It is a mollusc – a group of soft animals without backbones, such as clams and snails. Squid have highly developed nervous systems and superb eyesight. They communicate by rapidly changing skin colour.

Two long tenta with suckered tips seizing prey and ma

GREY STARFISH ▶
Starfish are not fish at all, but echinoderms, spiny-skinned animals with a central mouth and up to 40 arms. Instead of a single brain they have nerves along the arms, and if an arm is lost a new one soon takes its place. Starfish are predators, feeding on mussels and other shellfish.

Papulae (fleshy lobes) help the starfish to breathe

▲ PARROTFISH
The parrotfish is named after its teeth, which resemble a hard beak. It is vegetarian, nibbling algae from coral surfaces. At night, some species of parrotfish spin a bag of slimy mucus around their bodies. This bag prevents their scent from trailing through the water and stops predators from attacking them in their sleep.

▲ CORAL REEF
Corals are communities of many small individuals called polyps. Each polyp has a soft body in a limestone tube and is permanently fixed to other polyps to form rounded, branching, or fan-like structures attached to rock. The polyps are nourished by algae living on their surface. The algae need sunlight to survive, so corals are commonly found in shallow, inshore waters.

▲ LOBSTER
The lobster is a crustacean with a hard, jointed shell and four pairs of walking legs. A fifth pair of legs is modified into a pair of powerful claws. The lobster hides in a lair on a sandy or rocky sea-bed, waiting for its prey. Almost anything is on the menu, from small fish to other lobsters as well as plants.

Mantle is a thick, muscular sheath covering organs

Eight true arms with suckers along their length

PLANKTON

MYSID SHRIMP
Mysid shrimps are small crustaceans that live in open seas as well as coastal and freshwater habitats. They swarm in vast numbers, filtering tiny particles of food from the water. The females keep their babies in a pouch for several weeks. Mysids are an important prey item for many fish species.

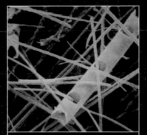

PHYTOPLANKTON
Phytoplankton are tiny, simple organisms, halfway between plant and animal. They survive only in the sunlit zone, where they absorb nutrients from the seawater, and are more common closer to shore than in the open sea. Vast quantities of phytoplankton drift in the currents, forming a living soup on which zooplankton feed.

COPEPOD
Copepods are zooplankton – tiny, swarming animals. Like shrimp, copepods are crustaceans. They have hard shells and many legs. There are over 7,500 copepod species, and their populations number in billions. They feed on phytoplankton and are a source of food for shoaling fishes such as herring.

▲ CONTINENTAL MARGIN
When a continent meets an ocean, the gently sloping sea-bed has an average depth of 130 m (430 ft) before falling away steeply farther offshore. This area, known as the continental margin, occupies a small fraction of the total ocean area, but provides some of the richest habitats for sea life, including crustaceans. This is especially true in cooler latitudes, where currents bring nutrients up from nearby deeper water.

▲ VIPERFISH
In the dark ocean depths, a hunter has no chance of chasing prey. Prey must be seized at once, or lost. The viperfish has a loose-hinged lower jaw and stretchy stomach for taking in large prey, and its spine-like teeth are angled back to allow no escape. Some species produce light to lure prey near.

▲ OPEN SEA
The open sea lacks a rich source of nutrients and is the poorest of ocean habitats. Its most numerous life-forms are plankton – tiny, simple plants and animals, which include fish and crustacean larvae. On the seafloor there is too little light and too much pressure for most life-forms. However, enough organic material sinks down to nourish deep-sea forms of starfish and worms.

OCEANS

The oceans cover more than 70 per cent of Earth's surface, to an average depth of 3.8 km (2.4 miles). They are home to more than a quarter of a million known plant and animal species. Six times as many land species are known to science, so it is likely that many more ocean species are still to be discovered when we find the means to explore its depths. Oceans shape our lives. They provide food, water, medicines, industrial materials, and energy, they stabilize Earth's turbulent atmosphere, and they provide transport and recreation. Without them there might not be any life.

◄ SUNLIT ZONE
Most fish, turtles, and other large marine animals are found in the uppermost 200 m (660 ft), the sunlit or photic zone. The most numerous life-forms here are the plankton – tiny animals and plant-like organisms that drift in the water. They photosynthesize (use sunlight and nutrients to make energy), and are the most important source of protein in marine food webs.

◄ TWILIGHT ZONE
The twilight zone extends to depths of about 1,000 m (3,300 ft). Many midwater animals, such as herring and squid, rise to the surface at night to prey on plankton, then sink to deeper waters by day. The sperm whale, one of the giants of the twilight zone, illustrates how the buoyancy of seawater allows ocean creatures to grow to greater size than land animals, which have the problem of supporting their weight.

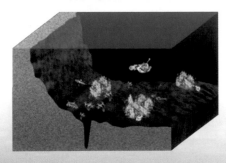

◄ DEEP-SEA ZONE
The ocean deep is very cold, salty, and pitch-black. Its few fish tend to be small. Hunters, such as viperfish, produce chemical light to lure prey close to their mouths. The sea-bed crawls with worms, which feed on the drizzle of organic debris raining down from above. On deep sea-beds, nutrients bubble up from volcanic hot springs, supporting a few organisms that do not depend on oxygen.

▲ SALT EVAPORATING PONDS
Crystallized salt at the ocean's edge is formed by evaporation of seawater. The 3.5% salt content of seawater comes from minerals containing chlorine and sodium that are dissolved from rocks on land and then carried down rivers to the sea. Undersea volcanoes also pump minerals into the water. Producing sea salt from the ocean is a major industry.

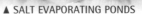

oceans

GLOBAL OCEAN CURRENTS

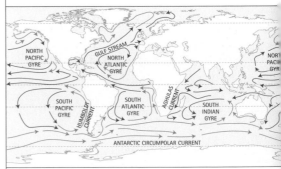

Water continuously moves through all the world's oceans. The Great Ocean Conveyor is a circulation belt that starts with cold polar water sinking in the North Atlantic. The cold water flows deep down, stirring up sea-bed nutrients. It makes the return journey warmed by tropical Sun. Upwellings of deep water form cold, nutrient-rich currents off the west coasts of the Americas and Africa. Ocean gyres are circular flows created by winds on the surface. In the Southern Ocean, constant west-to-east currents are driven by storm winds.

THE EXPANSE OF THE OCEAN ►
The world has 5 major oceans: Pacific, Atlantic, Indian, Arctic, and Southern, in descending order of size. Each ocean is fringed by seas that cut into the land margins. The ocean looks flat and featureless, but immense mountains rise from the floor. Volcanoes and ridges pour out lava where oceanic plates meet. Trenches in the ocean floor reach depths of more than 11 km (6.8 miles). The oceans contain some 1.37 billion km³ (329 million cu miles) of water.

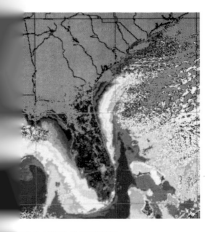

◄ GULF STREAM, FLORIDA
On a satellite map of Florida, the warm waters of the Gulf Stream (orange) show up against the blue-greys of normal sea temperatures. The Gulf Stream is a Sun-warmed current that flows from the Caribbean Sea up the USA's Atlantic coast, stirring up nutrients from the sea-bed and affecting the local climate. Part of the current then heads east to warm Britain, while the rest continues as a gyre, or circular current, around the North Atlantic.

ING THE OCEANS

FISHING FOR FOOD
The oceans are our top source of wild protein, with up to 80 million tonnes (78.6 million tons) of seafood caught each year. Key catches include herring, anchovy, cod, hake, and haddock. Some 2 million tonnes of seaweed are harvested annually to produce foods such as ice cream, as well as medicines. But widespread overfishing means that many fish stocks are now falling.

TRANSPORT
It is 10 times cheaper to ship goods by sea than by truck, and 3 times cheaper than by rail. Today, huge cargo vessels ply the oceans laden with cargoes such as crude oil and metal ores. The world's largest oil tanker, *Jahre Viking*, carries more than half a million tonnes of crude oil. Ship canals, such as the Suez and Panama canals, provide short-cuts between seas and oceans.

ENERGY
The oceans are rich in energy: nearly a third of today's petroleum and natural gas production is from beneath the ocean floor. Depths of up to 2,500 m (8,200 ft) can be reached from ship-mounted drills, although deep drilling is a costly business. Other sources of ocean energy include wave and tidal power, in which the movement of water is converted to electricity through the use of turbines, stationed at sea.

▲ BOAT ON ROUGH SEAS
Storms like these have claimed many lives since humans first went to sea, but they are all part of the water cycle. Water evaporates from the ocean's surface to form storm clouds and unstable air, leading to high winds. Clouds carry the water vapour over land and give us rain. Despite the violence of storms, ocean waters heat up and cool down less rapidly than land, so they help keep the temperature of the atmosphere stable.

Long, narrow, straight wings are ideal for soaring

▲ OCEAN ALBATROSS
The Southern Ocean is home to the wandering albatross *Diomedea exulans*. Its vast wingspan, up to nearly 3.5 m (11 ft), enables it to soar for literally years on end on the constant winds. Landing only to breed on remote cliffs, the albatross may cover 6,000 km (3,700 miles) in less than 2 weeks. It drops to the surface to pluck fish and squid from the water, but also follows fishing boats for scraps.

WAVES AND TSUNAMIS

Waves are a visible sign of energy moving through surface waters. The energy comes from wind on the water, and the more wind, the larger the waves. Ocean waves break as they reach the shore, shaping coastlines through erosion. Wave power offers us a clean source of energy. But waves are also dangerous and can capsize ocean-going vessels during severe storms. The deadliest of all waves are tsunamis: shockwaves triggered by seafloor movements that accompany volcanic eruptions and earthquakes and by large landslides into the sea. Tsunamis can travel at speeds of up to 950 kph (590 mph) and wreak devastation on coastal settlements.

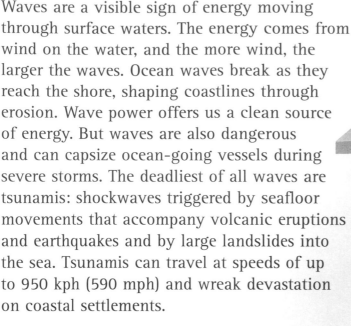

Winds blowing over the ocean surface cause water particles to travel in circles

Circles are most powerful at the surface, but fade out at greater depths

Top of water breaks to form a crest, whic crashes onto the sho

Shallow water bed slows the wave at its base

▲ WAVE ACTION
As wave energy advances, it causes water to rotate in circles, or orbits. The uppermost orbits show on the surface as rounded waves, or swell. The wave creates orbits down to a depth of half the wavelength (the distance between two crests). When a wave enters shallows, the deeper orbits drag on the beach and slow the wave's base. Waves become more closely packed. They steepen and form sharp crests, which eventually collapse into breakers.

Face: front wall of wave

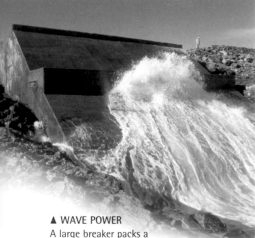

▲ WAVE POWER
A large breaker packs a punch of well over a thousand tonnes per square centimetre, and in theory the tides and waves offer an endless source of energy. Tidal power stations work by directing the water flow through turbines, which generate electricity. But these are only truly effective where the tidal range (distance in height between high and low tide) is at least 5 m (16 ft), and fewer than 50 sites worldwide offer the right conditions.

LARGE BREAKING WAVE ▶
The biggest ocean waves break on Maui, Hawaii, where some exceed 18 m (60 ft) in height. The Pacific Ocean delivers the biggest breakers because it has the longest fetch – the distance over which wind can blow. The greater the fetch, the greater the wave. Wave energy can travel immense distances; one study tracked swell all the way up the Pacific from Antarctica to the Aleutian Islands, a distance of more than 10,000 km (6,210 miles).

Trough: deepest point between two waves

Reducing water depth slows tsunami

Nearer shore, decreasing depth has a braking effect on the wave

Tsunami grows higher and higher before it finally breaks

◀ TSUNAMI
A violent crustal movement may send a wave – a tsunami – across oceans at incredible speeds. At first the wave may be only a metre (40 in) or so high and its wavelength extremely long. As the water gets shallower, the bottom of the waves brakes sharply, but the top continues to push forward, until it topples with tremendous force on the shore.

	Speed kph (mph)	950 (590)	710 (440)	500 (310)	150 (93)	40 (25)
Sea level (still water level)	Depth m (ft)	7,000 (23,000)	4,000 (13,120)	2,000 (6,560)	200 (3,280)	10 (33)

Submarine earthquake creates shockwave

Fault movement

tsunamis

Crest: *peak of wave or top of wave height*

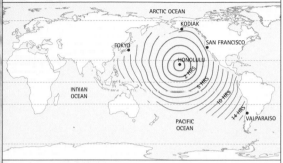

◄ HILO, HAWAII

Tsunamis cause a lot of the fatalities attributed to earthquakes and volcanoes. A tsunami that swept Hilo, Hawaii, on 1 April, 1946, was generated by an earthquake near Unimak, Alaska. Less than five hours later, with no warning, several waves up to 14 m (46 ft) high hit the northeast coast of Hawaii. More than 170 people, including the man in this picture, lost their lives. The Tsunami Warning System (TWS) was set up in response to this disaster.

TSUNAMI RISK AREA

A tsunami can form a broad front that crosses oceans in a few hours. The Hawaiian island chain is most at risk from earthquakes originating along the line of volcanic activity that encircles the Pacific Ocean, known as the "Ring of Fire". After the 1946 tsunami, the US established the Tsunami Warning System (TWS). Based in Honolulu, Hawaii, the TWS generates computer-calculated risk reports. The circular lines on the map are estimates of the time it would take for a wave originating near Valparaiso to reach Honolulu.

Deforested slopes show how high the wave rose

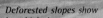

◄ LITUYA BAY, ALASKA

Lituya Bay, Alaska, was the location of the largest wave ever known. On 9 July, 1958, an earthquake measuring 7.9 on the Richter Scale struck at the head of Lituya Bay. The tremor caused a landslide into the bay. In one giant mass, 90 million tonnes of rock fell into the water. The resulting splash wave reached heights of 520 m (1,700 ft) on the surrounding hillsides, snapping trees as though they were matchsticks.

▲ OKUSHIRI, JAPAN

On 12 July, 1993, a seafloor earthquake off Hokkaido, Japan, created a tsunami that a few minutes later swept nearby Okushiri Island. It killed 120 people and caused US$600 billion worth of damage. Most of the waves reached heights of 15–20 m (50–65 ft), but in one location a valley concentrated the force of the wave, which peaked at a height of more than 30 m (100 ft) and washed away an entire village. Stores of heating fuels caught fire and burned down 340 homes.

EL NINO

Tropical winds and warm ocean currents in the Pacific Ocean usually flow from east to west. But once in every two to seven years the flow reverses, and warm water moves from west to east. Known as El Niño, the reversal brings misery to millions of people by triggering floods, droughts, famine, and disease outbreaks in the Pacific area. Scientists are not sure what causes El Niño, but it coincides with the Southern Oscillation, a reversal in atmospheric pressure in the Pacific. The two effects are so closely linked that they are often simply named the El Niño–Southern Oscillation, or ENSO.

▲ PERUVIAN FISHERMEN
Fishermen in Peru named El Niño, meaning "the child", after the Christ child, because it occurs around Christmas. Their livelihood depends on the cold current that normally flows past the coast. In El Niño years the warm countercurrent is poor in nutrients. The fish starve, or leave the area, and fishing is poor.

▲ FLOODING ON THE CALIFORNIAN COAST
Some El Niño years are more severe than others, and weather patterns may be disrupted over a wide area. In 1997–98, one of the worst El Niño seasons on record, fierce storms battered the coast of California. They washed away coastlines and flooded beachfront properties, causing around US$550 million worth of damage. That same year, torrential rainfall brought on by disturbed weather patterns also caused floods and landslides across the southern United States.

◄ DROUGHTS IN INDONESIA
An Indonesian farmer picks the last of his parched crop. Low atmospheric pressure over the warm western Pacific Ocean usually brings heavy rainfall to Indonesia, northern Australia, and the Philippines. But during an El Niño year, the eastward flow of warm water takes the rainfall with it, leaving the western Pacific high and dry. In 1997, droughts across Indonesia led to uncontrollable forest fires and crop failures.

El Nino

MONITORING EL NINO
After the 1997–98 El Niño, which killed an estimated 23,000 people, US scientists set up a network of weather buoys across the Pacific. Scientific research into the workings of the atmosphere and ocean currents may help meteorologists make long-term forecasts, vital aid in preparing for drought and flood.

Elevated areas
*of warm water
shown in red*

SATELLITE IMAGING ▶
Ocean temperature can be monitored from space, because warm water expands and creates slight "hills" on the surface. A satellite emits radar signals that bounce off the ocean and accurately measure the distance between the surface and the satellite. This satellite radar image of the Pacific during the El Niño effect reveals a vast zone of warm water (shown as red/yellow) in the eastern Pacific, where normally there would be cold currents (blue/green).

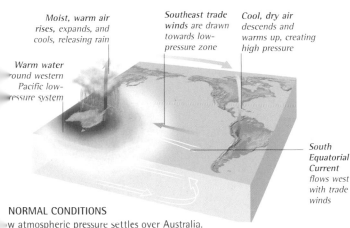

Moist, warm air rises, expands, and cools, releasing rain

Southeast trade winds are drawn towards low-pressure zone

Cool, dry air descends and warms up, creating high pressure

Warm water around western Pacific low-pressure system

South Equatorial Current flows west with trade winds

NORMAL CONDITIONS
Low atmospheric pressure settles over Australia. Warm ocean waters evaporate, and the moist air expands and rises, then cools and releases rain. Meanwhile, atmospheric pressure in the east is high. Cold ocean currents sweep the South American coast. The difference in atmospheric pressure draws the trade winds (tropical winds) to the northwest. The winds sustain the South Equatorial Current, in which warm water flows west.

Cool, dry air descends and creates high pressure

Trade winds reverse direction, heading east

Ocean current reverses, and warm countercurrent flows east

Warm waters off South America feed low-pressure system

▲ EL NIÑO EFFECT
The ENSO effect throws the whole system into reverse. The Southern Oscillation creates high pressure over the western Pacific and low pressure off South America. In these conditions, the trade winds falter and even blow back to the east. The surface waters of the central and eastern Pacific warm up. They generate a huge tongue of warm water that flows east to South America and displaces the usual cold currents.

▲ FISH STOCKS MOVE TO OTHER AREAS
During an El Niño, the warm waters that wash the South American coasts disrupt marine ecosystems. With no cold currents, there is no upwelling of nutrients to feed the plankton. Small fish that eat plankton, such as anchovy, pilchard, and herring, die in their thousands. Others migrate elsewhere.

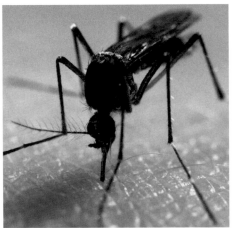

▲ MOSQUITO INCREASE BRINGS DISEASE
Changes in rainfall, temperature, and humidity caused by El Niño can lead to the spread of disease. Mosquitoes thrive in the higher temperatures, infecting people with malaria and dengue. Other diseases linked with El Niño include hepatitis, yellow fever, and cholera.

▲ COASTAL DAMAGE
The 1997–98 El Niño produced an immense pool of warm water in the east Pacific. Its effects were felt far beyond South America. In Oregon on the northeast Pacific coast, water levels rose up to 60 cm (2 ft) above normal. The warm water stayed in the area for years, causing storms and landslides.

EXPLORING OCEAN DEPTHS

Deep water is near-freezing, pitch-dark, and under immense pressure, so it is no surprise that the ocean depths remain the last great unexplored region on Earth. Until the 20th century humans could barely dive more than a few metres down, let alone reach the ocean floor's limit at 11 km (7 miles). Today, scientists use manned or unmanned submersibles (small submarines) to get a close-up view of the deep and gather samples. Ships use sonar instruments and satellite location devices to make maps of the ocean floor.

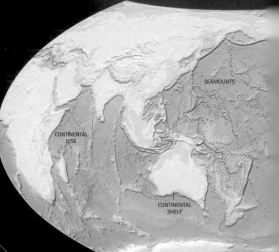

JOHNSON SUBMERSIBLE ▶
This Johnson Sea Link carries a pilot and a scientist to depths of more than 900 m (3,000 ft), and collects samples. The Shinkai 6500, a manned Japanese craft, has reached depths six times greater; in theory it can survey 98% of the world's oceans. The manned depth record was set in 1960 when the *Trieste* went to the bottom of the Mariana Trench, the deepest point of any ocean at 10,911 m (35,800 ft).

◀ MODERN ROBOT SUBMERSIBLE
Robot submersibles are unmanned vehicles used in places that are too confined or too deep to use manned craft safely. Some are no larger than shoe-boxes. Remotely operated vehicles (ROVs) are controlled by cable from a ship, whereas autonomously operated vehicles (AOVs) direct themselves and are programmed by on-board computers. In 1986 the ROV *Alvin* explored the wreck of the *Titanic* in 3,800 m (12,460 ft) of water off the US coast.

Computer program creates three-dimensional map from sonar readings

▲ SURVEY SHIP USING SONAR
Scientists use sonar to map the ocean floor. An instrument on or near the surface beams a sound pulse at a wide strip of sea-bed, then records how long the sound takes to return. From the time readings, depths can be calculated, then turned into three-dimensional computer maps of the ocean floor. Other sonar instruments, towed very near the ocean floor, pick up detailed features on it, such as mineral growths.

SEAMOUNTS

CONTINENTAL RISE

CONTINENTAL SHELF

MAP OF OCEAN FLOOR ▲
This ocean floor map was produced by US scientists Marie Tharp and Bruce Heezen. From the late 1940s they mapped the North Atlantic, and in 1957 produced the first of many maps of the ocean floor. For the first time, scientists saw volcanoes, mid-ocean ridges, and valleys, which marked the boundaries between spreading oceanic plates. The new maps provided evidence for the theory of plate tectonics, which was not widely accepted until the 1960s.

▲ OCEAN FLOOR

Where continents meet the ocean, the ocean floor deepens to the edge of the continental shelf. The steep continental slope gives way to flat abyssal plains. Great ridges of basalt form at the boundaries of spreading oceanic plates. Where an oceanic plate is subducted (sinks down) beneath a continental plate, a deep trench forms on the ocean floor.

(1) *Continental shelf:* shallowly sloping ocean floor at margin of continent

(2) *Continental slope:* steep slope to ocean floor

(3) *Submarine canyon:* formed by erosion

(4) *Continental rise:* gentle slope between abyssal plain and continental slope

(5) *Abyssal plain:* flat ocean floor covered by thin sediment

(6) *Seamount:* submarine volcanic peak

(7) *Guyot:* submarine volcano with an eroded summit

(8) *Mid-oceanic ridge:* basalt build-up at diverging plate boundary

(9) *Trench:* formed at subduction zone

(10) *Island arc:* volcanic islands formed above subduction zone

HYDROTHERMAL VENT ▶

Hydrothermal vents are sea-bed hot springs created when seawater contacts hot volcanic rock, then flows back to the sea-bed. The hot springs are also called "black smokers", owing to the colour of suspended minerals in the hot water. Bacteria make sugars for food from carbon dioxide. They are the base of a food chain for more than 300 species, including worms up to 3 m (10 ft) long that live around the vents. Vents were first discovered off the Galapagos Islands in 1977.

_____ *"Black smoker"* of sulphurous hot water

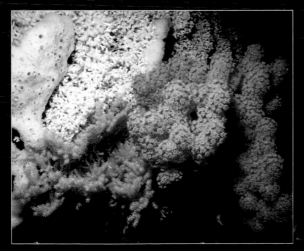

▲ DEEPWATER CORAL

Corals usually grow in warm, shallow waters. But scientists using robot submersibles in the North Atlantic and Pacific have filmed cold-water coral reefs at temperatures of 4–12°C (39–54°F) and depths of 3,000 m (9,840 ft). The corals feed by trapping food particles from the water. Most other corals rely on algae living on the reefs to help them build their skeletons. Some governments are writing laws to protect their cold-water reefs from damage by fishing.

MID-OCEANIC RIDGE

CONTINENTAL SLOPE

ocean depths

ATMOSPHERE

The atmosphere is an envelope of gases surrounding Earth. It is composed almost entirely of nitrogen, oxygen, and argon, with minute traces of water vapour and other gases. The atmosphere gives us air to breathe and provides water to drink in the form of rain. It protects us from the more harmful energy given out by the Sun, but also traps the Sun's warmth and keeps surface temperatures relatively stable. Without it we would either freeze or burn to a crisp as Earth rotates.

▲ EARTH'S ATMOSPHERE
The view from space reveals the atmosphere as a light haze around the planet. Although it has no upper limit, blending seamlessly into the vacuum of space, it is only in the lowest 100 km (62 miles) that atmospheric density is great enough to screen out harmful solar radiation. The atmosphere makes Earth unique in the Solar System: it is the only planet surrounded by gases that can sustain life.

atmosphere

ATMOSPHERE LAYERS ▶
The atmosphere divides into four unequal layers on the basis of temperature. The outer layer, the thermosphere, is the thickest, extending up to 500 km (310 miles) into space, and is cold at the bottom and very hot at the top. The lowest layer, the troposphere, is only 16 km (10 miles) thick. This layer is warmed by solar heat, and churns with turbulent weather. It contains dust and soil particles, ash from volcanoes, and – increasingly – polluting chemicals.

Satellites operate way above the atmosphere in space

120 km
75 miles

110 km
68 miles

Aurora occurs i the thermospher

100 km
62 miles

90 km
56 miles

80 km
50 miles

70 km
43 miles

60 km
37 miles

50 km
31 miles

40 km
25 miles

Thin layer o ozone absorb harmful radiatio

30 km
19 miles

Jet airliners fly at about 10 km (6 miles) high, in the troposphere

20 km
12 miles

10 km
6 miles

Sea level

Height above sea level

▲ DARK CLOUD AND RAIN
The atmosphere is an active element in the water cycle. Water evaporates from the surface of oceans and lakes; the warmer the air, the more water vapour it can hold. The vapour is transported by air currents to the land, where it rises, cools, forms clouds, and falls as rain. The percentage of water vapour in the atmosphere varies: desert air contains almost no vapour at all, whereas the moist air of the humid tropics may hold up to 4% water vapour.

▲ SMOG OVER HELSBY, CHESHIRE, UK
Pollution from the factory chimneys creates a smog cloud over this English landscape. Smog contains ozone, which is a form of oxygen whose molecules contain three atoms, unlike the usual two in the oxygen we normally breathe. It occurs mostly in the stratosphere. However, airborne industrial pollutants, such as nitrogen oxides and hydrocarbons, can create ozone at ground level when they react together in the presence of sunlight. Ozone is poisonous, causing lung damage.

▲ OZONE HOLE, 2003
This coloured satellite image shows low atmospheric ozone levels over Antarctica. The ozone hole (dark blue) is 28.2 km² (10.9 sq miles) in size, although it has reduced slightly since 2000 and is predicted to decline over future years. Ozone protects Earth's surface from harmful ultraviolet radiation.

▲ STORMY SEA
Stormy winds are the product of an active atmosphere. Uneven heating of Earth's surface results in an unequal distribution of air pressure. This creates wind, a horizontal movement of air from an area of high pressure to an area of low pressure. The most violent winds – hurricanes – are created when a very large mass of warm, moist air rises. This creates a low-pressure area below, into which air rushes at high speed.

▲ METEOR BARRIER
The atmosphere is not solid, but it acts like a massive, soft wall on meteors and other space rocks. Every day, thousands hurtle through the vacuum of space towards Earth. Friction – the rubbing of the atmosphere on their surface – causes them to burn up before they strike. Only a few are large enough to reach Earth's surface, and even fewer cause damage. The violent effects of meteor strikes can be seen on the cratered surface of the Moon, which has no atmosphere.

60°C
140°F

-10°C
14°F

-80°C
-112°F

Thermosphere
The outermost layer fades into the vacuum of space.

-90°C
-130°F

meteor burns up
[du]e to friction in
[th]e atmosphere

-80°C
-112°F

[no]ctilucent clouds,
[fo]rmed from ice
[cr]ystals on meteor
[d]ust, in the upper
[m]esosphere

Mesosphere
In the mesosphere, temperatures drop as the altitude increases. This layer contains very little water vapour. Its lower limit is called the stratopause or mesopeak, and its upper limit is the mesopause.

-50°C
-58°F

-30°C
-22°F

-10°C
14° F

Stratosphere
The stratosphere is important for its ozone layer at an altitude of about 25 km (16 miles). This layer absorbs ultraviolet radiation from the Sun that would otherwise reach the ground and harm us. Above the ozone layer, radiation causes temperatures in the stratosphere to increase.

-20°C
-4°F

-40°C
-40°F

Weather is
[r]estricted to the
[t]roposphere, the
[l]owest level of the
[a]tmosphere

-60°C
-76°F

-60°C
-76°F

Troposphere
The troposphere is the layer in which we live. The large temperature changes cause mixing of the air, which we experience as weather.

15°C
59°F

Average temperature

◀ **EXTREME COLD**
Climate affects people's way of life. Few people choose to live in cold climates, but those who do have come to depend on it. The Inuit people of the Arctic, who use native animals for transport, food, and clothing, developed such customs from long experience of the local climate. During the winter they hunt seal and walrus from ice on the ocean.

Inuit wears layers of animal furs to keep out cold

Reindeer are used for food, clothing, and transport

Equator

CLIMATE CHANGE

Earth's climates result from interactions of the Sun, the atmosphere, Earth, and the watery part of Earth's surface – especially the oceans. We use the word climate to describe how we expect the weather to behave in any place. Climates vary from one region to the next because of differences in sunlight, temperature, rainfall, winds, ocean currents, and land shapes. Climate also changes on a global scale. In the past, Earth has been both warmer and colder than today. Scientists suspect that we may now be helping warm the world's climate by adding carbon dioxide to the atmosphere through burning coal, oil, and natural gas.

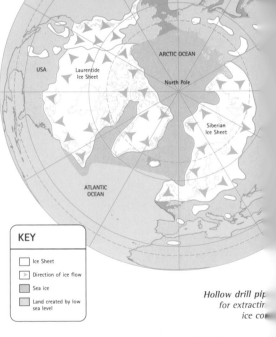

PACIC OCEAN

ARCTIC OCEAN

USA

Laurentide Ice Sheet

North Pole

Siberian Ice Sheet

ATLANTIC OCEAN

KEY

☐ Ice Sheet
▷ Direction of ice flow
☐ Sea ice
☐ Land created by low sea level

Camel allows its body temperature to rise by day, then loses excess heat at night

Cover-up clothing defends against the Sun's fierce heat and sandstorms

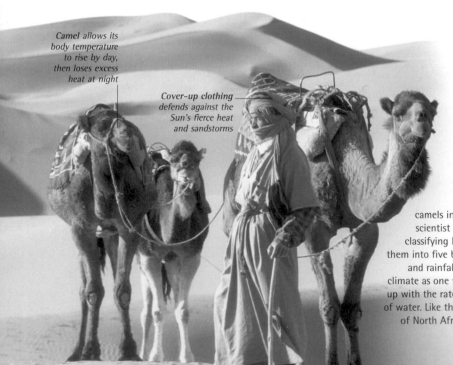

Hollow drill pip for extractir ice co

◀ **EXTREME HEAT**
Here, a Tuareg camel herder tends his camels in the North African desert. The German scientist Wladimir Köppen invented a system of classifying Earth's many different climates. He put them into five broad groups according to temperature and rainfall. Köppen's system describes the desert climate as one where the rate of rainfall cannot catch up with the rate of evaporation: there is always a lack of water. Like the Inuit in the Arctic, the Tuareg people of North Africa – and the camel – have adapted to survive in an extreme climate.

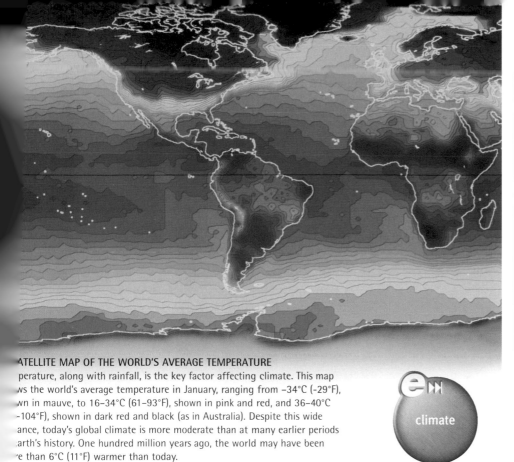

SATELLITE MAP OF THE WORLD'S AVERAGE TEMPERATURE
Temperature, along with rainfall, is the key factor affecting climate. This map shows the world's average temperature in January, ranging from −34°C (-29°F), shown in mauve, to 16–34°C (61–93°F), shown in pink and red, and 36–40°C (97–104°F), shown in dark red and black (as in Australia). Despite this wide variance, today's global climate is more moderate than at many earlier periods in Earth's history. One hundred million years ago, the world may have been more than 6°C (11°F) warmer than today.

climate

DRILLING FOR DEEP-SEA SEDIMENT CORE ▲
Scientists retrieve a core of sediment from the ocean floor. Sea-bed samples are a useful record of Earth's climate history. For example, they contain layers of microscopic fossils that are sensitive to sea temperatures, and are therefore good indicators of past climate change. Rock fragments carried out to sea and dumped by icebergs reveal where and when glaciers were active on land.

◀ EXTENT OF THE LAST GLACIATION
During the last Ice Age, which ended 10,000–15,000 years ago, ice covered 30% of the land. The North Polar icecap grew to cover 19 million km² (7.3 million sq miles) of North America, Siberia, and Europe. (The southern icecap was restricted to the land mass of Antarctica, as today.) Sea levels fell, having supplied the water vapour that created the snow and ice. The lowering sea levels exposed new areas of land on the margins of continents. These included a land bridge between North America and Siberia.

Clouds of volcanic ash erupting from Mount St Helens in 1980

sample taken depths up to m (11,800 ft)

◀ GEOLOGISTS STUDYING ICE CORE
Glaciations occur when low global temperatures create greater ice cover. Geologists study ice core samples to learn when, and for how long, glaciations took place. For example, the last Ice Age began 3 million years ago and consisted of 20 glaciations spaced about 100,000 years apart. Ancient ice reveals other clues about climate. Each layer preserves carbon dioxide and methane gas, dust, volcanic ash, and pollen, forming a record of the atmosphere at that time. The oldest known glaciation occurred about 2.3 billion years ago.

VOLCANIC ASH FROM MOUNT ST HELENS ▲
Erupting volcanoes send millions of tonnes of ash and gas, including sulphur dioxide, into the atmosphere. The sulphur dioxide gas mixes with water vapour to make clouds of very tiny droplets of sulphuric acid. These scatter sunlight back into space, causing Earth's surface to cool. Huge eruptions, like that of Tambora in Indonesia in 1815, can cool global temperatures for more than a year.

Deep, dark cumulonimbus clouds form as cold air forces moist warm air upwards

Cold front forms as cold air pushes against warm air

◄ ADVANCING COLD FRONT OVER FLORIDA
An aerial view shows a cold, high-pressure air mass (lower ri... moving into a warm, low-pressure air mass (upper left). Whe... cold mass invades a warm mass, the boundary is called a col... front. Clouds of different types form along the front, the lin... where they meet. A deep bank of cumulonimbus clouds sho... where dense cold air is forcing lighter warm air to rise steep... and shed water vapour.

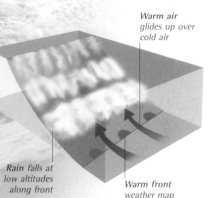

Warm air glides up over cold air

◄ WARM FRONT
When a warm air mass advances after a retreating cold air mass, the boundar... between them is termed a warm front. The cold air si... to the ground and the war... air moves overhead, so the... front becomes a shallow sl... The warm air cools as it m... the slope, creating a range... cloud forms. The lowest cl... release moderate rainfall.

Rain falls at low altitudes along front

Warm front weather map symbol

WEATHER

Our everyday weather is controlled by the local behaviour of the atmosphere. Warm spells, dull days, and sudden cold showers all result from the movement of air masses. Large air masses typically have a uniform temperature and air pressure, so they may bring several days of stable weather while passing overhead. But when two different air masses collide, a change in weather occurs along the boundary, or front, between them. The factors that affect air pressure and movement range from the height of local mountain ranges to global wind and ocean currents.

COLD FRONT ►
When a cold air mass advances rapidly into a warm mass, the front is steeply sloped, and the warm air is forced to rise quickly. If the rising air is moist, water condenses from it to form towering cumulonimbus clouds. The energy circulating in the clouds produces thunderstorms and heavy, but brief, rainfall.

Cold air pushes war... air upwards

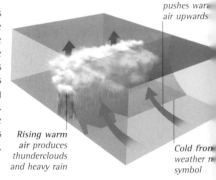

Rising warm air produces thunderclouds and heavy rain

Cold fron... weather m... symbol

◄ OCCLUDED FRONT
Occluded means "trapped", and this occurs when a warm front advances into cool air but is then overtaken by a cold front. The cold front wheels round behind and pushes up the warm air mass, which sheds heavy rainfall. Th... new, occluded front is formed between the three air masses.

Occluded front weather map symbol

Cold air catches up with warm air

Rising warm air sheds heavy rain

GLOBAL MOVEMENT OF WINDS

POLAR EASTERLIES
WESTERLIES
SW MONSOON
NE TRADES
NE TRADES
NE TRADES
DOLDRUMS
DOLDRUMS
DOLDRUMS
SE TRADES
SE TRADES
SE TRADES
WESTERLIES
WESTERLIES
WESTERLIES
POLAR EASTERLIES

Winds blowing towards the equator are deflected west by Earth's rotation. These winds, known as the trades or trade winds, die down near the equator to create a still belt known as the doldrums. In the temperate zones, the prevailing winds are westerlies (blowing from the west), which are also governed by Earth's rotation. Cold, dry, easterly winds blow from the constant high-pressure zones over the North and South Poles. On large landmasses, the monsoon – a seasonal change in land and sea temperatures – leads to wet onshore winds in summer and dry offshore winds in winter.

WIND ►
Wind is the movement of air from colder, high-pressure zones to warmer, low-pressure zones. It reacts rapidly to a change in conditions, as can be seen on many coastlines. At night, the land cools more rapidly than the sea, so winds blow offshore from the cool to the warm zone. By day, the pressures are reversed. The land warms up more rapidly than the sea, creating low pressure and attracting onshore winds.

SAN FRANCISCO FOG
Some places experience their own local weather conditions. During summer, fog shrouds the San Francisco Bay. By day, the California valleys warm up and create an area of low pressure. This draws sea winds onshore. These warm winds are full of moisture from evaporated seawater. As they blow coastwards, they pass over surface waters chilled by the California Current. This cools the winds, causing moisture to condense out of them as fog.

Golden Gate Bridge, San Francisco, California

HOW MOUNTAINS AFFECT WEATHER

ALPS
Mountains strongly affect local weather conditions. High-pressure systems over mountains send cold winds rushing down the slopes into the valleys below. In southern France, the Mistral – a dry, icy wind from the Alps – funnels down the Rhône valley at high speed, and is a key weather-maker in France's Provence region.

FOREST FIRES
The mountains of southern California force winds to speed up as they pass overhead or are funnelled through narrow passes. By the time the winds descend the other side, they are drained of all moisture. Hot and dry, these Santa Ana winds parch the valley vegetation and seriously increase the risk of forest fires.

DESERT SNOW ▲
Weather is full of surprises, and can change dramatically from day to day. The Mojave desert in the southwest of North America bakes during the summer and receives less than 150 mm (6 in) of annual precipitation, but it is not a hot desert. It lies at high altitudes in a temperate zone. Temperatures may plummet to –13°C (9°F) in winter, and the vegetation, including the Joshua Tree yucca, has to be prepared for sudden snowfalls.

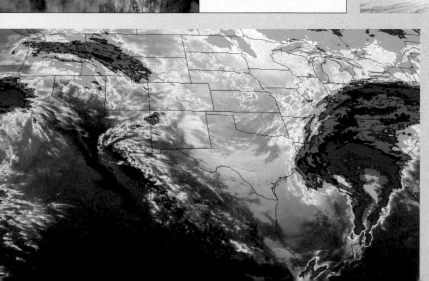

◄ SATELLITE WEATHER IMAGING
A satellite image shows atmospheric conditions over the USA. Spacecraft and radar are just two of the instruments used by meteorologists to analyse and forecast the weather. This service is vital: an estimated 80% of US national emergencies are linked to extreme weather conditions. As well as national forecasts, predictions are made for large cities, which give out so much heat and pollution that they create their own conditions.

PRECIPITATION

Precipitation is the name given to water and ice that collect on Earth's surface from the atmosphere. It is a feature of water's remarkable ability to transform rapidly between solid (ice), liquid (rain and dew), or gas (water vapour) within a narrow temperature range. Many parts of the world enjoy moderate rainfall, but some regions are permanently parched while others suffer disastrous floods. Where rain and snow fall, and for how long, depends a lot on location, season, and the shape of the land.

◄ RAIN

Rain is caused by the movement of air masses. When moist, warm air rises it expands, loses energy, and cools. Cool air can hold less moisture than warm air. So water condenses out of it in clouds of countless tiny droplets. Dust or ice crystals in the clouds collect water droplets and grow into raindrops. Many factors can make warm air create rain clouds. These include frontal wedging, convergence, and mountain lifting, which are illustrated below.

RAIN CLOUD FORMATION

FRONTAL WEDGING

Friction slows air near ground; air above flows faster, creating a wedge-shaped front

Warm air rises up wedge and cools, producing rain clouds

Warm, moist air masses converge and rise to form clouds

Rising air expands and cools; water condenses from air to produce rain

CONVERGENCE

MOUNTAIN LIFTING

Rising warm, moist air meets mountain, lifts, and sheds rain on near slopes

Far slopes are left dry

WORLD PRECIPITATION

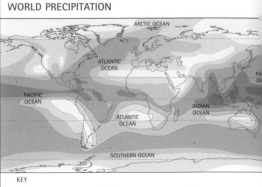

KEY

▮ 300 – 400 cm	▮ 100 – 200 cm	▮ 25 – 50 cm
▮ 200 – 300 cm	▮ 50 – 100 cm	▯ 0 – 25 cm

Tropical regions receive high rainfall because the ocean warmth leads to high evaporation, which increases the amount of moisture in the air. Polar regions are dry because cold air holds so little moisture. The large landmass of Asia creates low pressure during summer, which draws moist winds in from the ocean. High pressure in winter drives dry winds towards the ocean. This seasonal wind change is called the monsoon. Mountain ranges affect rainfall, too, by driving warm air upwards, which cools it, condenses water vapour, and creates rain.

DIFFERENT CLOUD TYPES

STRATUS
This term comes from a word meaning "layer" and describes clouds that form a more-or-less even layer. Like other cloud terms it can be used in combination. Nimbostratus is a grey layer of rain clouds at low altitude. Altostratus is a thinner, whiter layer at middle altitudes. Cirrostratus describes a thin, bright, high-altitude haze.

CUMULUS
Cumulus resembles a mass of rounded domes. Often the base is flat. These puffy clouds form at high altitude (cirrocumulus), mid-altitude (altocumulus), and low altitude (cumulus). These fluffy, "cotton-wool" clouds are characteristic of fair weather, but deep masses of cumulus with thick, dark bases are storm clouds and a sign of approaching rain.

CIRRUS
Cirrus clouds are very high, thin, and wispy, on account of the low water vapour content at high altitude. They consist of ice crystals and are a bright, reflective white. Some, known as mare's tails, look like fine strands of hair. Cirrus clouds do not themselves produce rain, but may be the first sign of an approaching warm front, promising rain later.

CUMULONIMBUS
Uprushing warm air masses can create towering clouds known as cumulonimbus up to 18 km (11 miles) deep. As the warm air rises and cools, it forms clouds and releases energy, and if it is still warmer than the surrounding air, it keeps moving upwards. Cumulonimbus clouds are a source of thunderstorms, and their upper levels may contain snow or hail.

SNOW

owflakes grow in clouds of super-cooled
our – water droplets that remain liquid way
w their normal freezing point. Super-cooled
our rapidly freezes onto any available surface,
hen ice crystals are present it clings to them,
ing them larger. As the flakes grow, gravity
es them fall. Snow reaches the ground only if
temperatures lower down remain cold. Snow
es are usually clumps of several ice crystals.

SNOW CRYSTAL

▼ THUNDER AND LIGHTNING

Thunderstorms are created by unstable air movements within
cumulonimbus clouds. Rain and hail move so vigorously that
they gather an electrical charge. Positive charges cluster high in
the cloud, while negative charges cluster lower down. When the
electrical resistance breaks down, lightning flashes between the
two within the cloud and sometimes between the cloud and the
ground. The thunder we hear is the sound of nearby air being
heated to temperatures of 20,000°C (36,000°F) – three times
hotter than the surface of the Sun. This compresses the
surrounding air, which produces a shock wave.

*Positively charged
hail and rain gather
in high cloud*

*New layer of
ice freezes
around the
hailstone*

*Raindrop
eezes into
hailstone*

*Hailstone is too
heavy to be held
in the cloud and
falls to the ground*

*Updraugh
carries
aindrop up*

Raindrop

Hailstone falls

*Negatively charged
hail and rain in low
cloud mass*

HOW HAIL FORMS

e snow, a hailstone starts life as a raindrop
a very cold cloud. But hail forms only in
ge clouds containing powerful updraughts of
nd. The hailstone first falls a little, collecting
oplets of super-cooled water vapour. Then
draughts carry the hailstone up again and
ore water vapour freezes onto it. This process
ntinues until the hailstone falls. Most hailstones
e pea-sized, but some are as big as oranges.

HUGE HAILSTONES

*Negative electrical
charge from cloud
leaps to positive
ground through
a lightning bolt*

precipitation

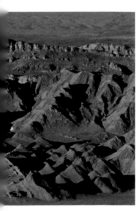

▲ ATACAMA IN CHILE

One of the world's driest
places is the Atacama desert in
Chile. The town of Iquique
receives heavy rain less than
5 times a century. The dry
conditions are due partly to
the Andes mountains.

▲ CHERRAPUNJI, INDIA

Some of the world's highest
rainfall is in the foothills of
the Himalayas and nearby
plateaus in northern India.
During the summer monsoon
(wind change), wet winds blow
north from the Indian Ocean.

*Ground is positively
charged and attracts
negative charge*

WEATHER FORECASTING

A timely warning of bad weather can save lives and property. Meteorology – the study of weather – is based on scientific observation of the atmosphere. Meteorologists collect readings of wind, temperature, pressure, and other conditions from weather stations on land and sea all over the world. The figures are analysed by powerful computers and shared between nations to produce the weather maps and forecasts we see on television. With modern technology, forecasters can predict weather several days into the future.

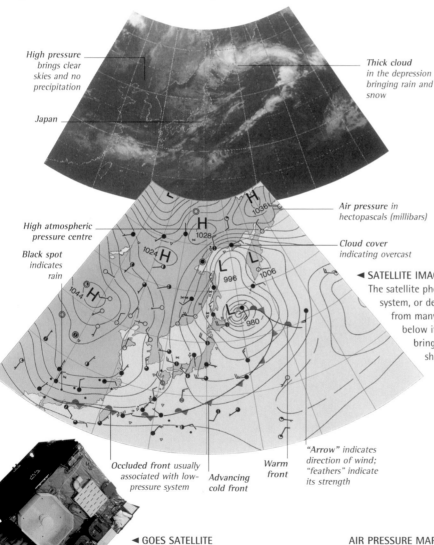

High pressure brings clear skies and no precipitation

Japan

Thick cloud in the depression bringing rain and snow

High atmospheric pressure centre

Black spot indicates rain

Air pressure in hectopascals (millibars)

Cloud cover indicating overcast

Occluded front usually associated with low-pressure system

Advancing cold front

Warm front

"Arrow" indicates direction of wind; "feathers" indicate its strength

▲ NSCAT IMAGE SHOWING TYPHOON ACTIVITY AROUND JAPAN
Radar signals from satellites and aircraft tell meteorologists about ocean wind conditions. This map of the Pacific shows fast winds in orange and slow winds in blue. The swirls near Japan are hurricanes or typhoons. Typhoon Violet, to the south, blew into Tokyo on 22 September, 1993, killing 3 people. The larger typhoon, Tom, headed east and blew out safely. The image was created by a scatterometer which sends radar signals from a satellite to the sea surface and "reads" the echoes that return. This image was gathered by a NASA Scatterometer (NSCAT) instrument on an weather satellite.

TYPHOON TOM

TYPHOON VIOLET

e ⯈⯈⯈ weather

◄ SATELLITE IMAGE AND CORRESPONDING WEATHER MAP
The satellite photograph and chart shows a developing low-pressure system, or depression, over Japan. The image, along with readings from many weather stations, helped meteorologists compose the weather map below it. Strong winds sweep anticlockwise around the low pressure centre, bringing warm and cold fronts with them. The symbols plotted on the map show weather fronts, surface conditions (such as rain), wind speed and direction, and air pressure.

◄ GOES SATELLITE
The US geostationary operational environmental satellite (GOES) remains in the same location above Earth. It measures atmospheric temperature, moisture, and winds, and also collects readings transmitted from weather buoys in the oceans. All the data is beamed down to Earth for analysis by the National Weather Service.

AIR PRESSURE MAP ►
Air pressure is the weight of the atmosphere over a unit area of Earth's surface. Changes of weather are usually accompanied by changes in air pressure so isobaric maps are needed for accurate weather forecasting. Isobars, the lines on a pressure map, connect points of equal pressure. The low-pressure centre shown here over the English Channel indicates high winds and heavy rain.

Close spacing of isobars indicates strong winds associated with low-pressure systems

High pressure centres bring light winds and settled dry weather

HIGH PRESSURE

HIGH PRESSURE

HIGH PRESSURE

LOW PRESSURE

HIGH PRESSURE

Long nose probe
samples air outside
the aircraft's influence

Trade winds (red)
to north and south
of equator

Anemometer *measures wind
speed and direction*

Solar panel *provides power
outside winter months*

▲ SNOOPY THE WEATHER PLANE

Weather aircraft serve an important role in sampling the atmosphere. *Snoopy*, a heavily modified Hercules transport plane, was used from 1972 to 2001 to conduct atmospheric research around the world. Its scientific instruments took a wide range of readings including atmospheric radiation, ozone, nitrogen content, and cloud density. The aircraft also released radio-sondes, probes that fell by parachute and sampled a vertical cross-section of the atmosphere.

◄ AUTOMATIC WEATHER STATION

Unmanned weather stations are especially useful in remote areas of the world. This is one of several automatic weather stations that record surface conditions on Antarctica. Some are positioned on icebergs in the ocean. Automatic weather stations measure temperature, pressure, humidity, and wind speed and direction. At regular intervals every day, they transmit readings via satellite to monitoring centres all over the world.

WEATHER BALLOON LAUNCH ►

An atmosphere researcher launches the daily weather balloon at his Antarctic base. The helium balloon carries a radiosonde, a sensor that takes a series of atmospheric readings as it rises. At an altitude of about 25 km (16 miles), low air pressure causes the balloon to burst, and the instrument returns to the ground by parachute. Balloon radiosondes are useful for measuring ozone in the upper atmosphere, enabling environmental change to be monitored.

Anemometer

▲ WEATHER BUOY

This is one of a network of moored weather buoys that operate in US waters. The buoys record wind and sea conditions in order to improve the accuracy of shipping forecasts and avert disasters such as coastal floods. Several countries run weather buoy networks. Along with data from satellites and weather stations, the buoy readings are transmitted over the Global Telecommunications System, an international network that shares weather data.

◄ WEATHER PLOTTING

At Bracknell, the headquarters of the UK Meteorological Office, computers combine data from weather recording stations in the UK. Surface readings are sent in by about 200 land stations and 600 ships and rigs, which form part of a 7,000-strong international fleet. Balloons and satellites provide upper-air readings, and a network of weather radars reports on rainfall. The computers provide nowcasting (short-term forecasts), as well as long-term forecasts.

TORNADOES

Tornadoes, also known as twisters, are the most violent of all winds, reaching speeds of up to 480 kph (300 mph). They take the form of a slender, whirling column, created when warm air is sucked into the zone of low air pressure beneath a thundercloud. A tornado releases immense energy as it tracks across the land, and can splinter houses or hurl trucks through the air. Though tornadoes strike many parts of the world, they are a particular menace on the North American prairies, where they kill around 60 people every year.

Tornado activity (marked in orange on this map) tends to occur in temperate regions, and in the central USA in particular, where the region from North Dakota south to Texas is known as "Tornado Alley". Tornadoes are common there in spring, when cold polar air meets warm, moist air from the Gulf of Mexico. The mixing air masses create cyclones, low-pressure zones where warm air rises in spirals. Throughout the northern hemisphere, tornadoes rotate anticlockwise, corresponding to the spin of cyclones. In the southern hemisphere, cyclones spin clockwise, and so do most tornadoes.

FORMATION OF A TORNADO

Funnel of visible cloud (water vapour) descends into column

Large air masses revolve, creating wide column of rotating air

Rotating air increases speed as column narrows

Rising warm air creates low pressure at ground level

Base of tornado causes localized destruction

Cone of water vapour

Dust stirred up by winds

1. FIRST SIGNS
It is widely thought that tornadoes touch down from a cloud to the ground. They do not. A mesocyclone (wide column of revolving air) already connects the cloud base and ground surface. Here, flying dust and a cone of cloud vapour are telltale signs of a mesocyclone.

Cooling air creates more water vapour

Faster winds stir more dust

2. COLUMN FORMS
The tornado is underway. As warm, moist air rushes into the base of the column and spirals upwards, it expands rapidly and cools. This causes it to release water vapour in the form of a cloud. It is the cloud, along with dust sucked up from below, that makes the column visible.

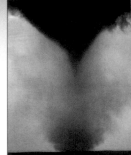

3. PEAK POWER
A tornado normally lasts a few minutes, but the strongest ones can last an hour or more. It decays when the supply of warm, moist air from the base runs out, or when draughts of cool, dry air sink from the cloud. The tornado often tightens into a slender rope of wind before dying away.

▲ **ANATOMY OF A TORNADO**
Warm, moist air rushes up into a big thundercloud known as a supercell, and rubs against cold air higher up. The two air masses turn around each other and create a mesocyclone – a wide column of revolving air. The mesocyclone spins faster as it sucks in more warm air. In about 50% of cases, the mesocyclone generates a really fast, destructive column of air – a tornado.

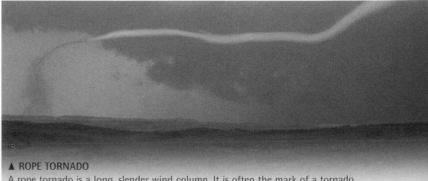

▲ **ROPE TORNADO**
A rope tornado is a long, slender wind column. It is often the mark of a tornado nearing the end of its life, though some tornadoes remain rope-like from start to finish. While rope tornadoes may roam erratically, they always remain attached to the storm cloud. They are no less destructive than wide tornadoes; in fact, as a column tightens, its wind speed increases, just as ice-skaters speed up as they draw up into a pirouette.

◄ TORNADO DAMAGE, USA, 1998
Tornadoes are the biggest threat to life and property in parts of the USA, destroying everything in their path. In the American Midwest, and particularly over the Mississippi valley, conditions are often right for tornadoes to develop. An extreme tornado, with winds over 450 kph (300 mph), can pick objects up and hurl them like bullets, strip a person's clothes off, or tear the roofs off houses, as shown here.

TRI-STATE TORNADO, 1925 ►
The longest-lasting and most destructive tornado in recorded history struck the US states of Missouri, Illinois, and Indiana on 18 March, 1925. The so-called Tri-State Tornado raced northeastwards for 352 km (219 miles) at speeds of up to 118 kph (73 mph), leaving a trail of devastation. It wiped out several villages, killed 695 people, and injured more than 2,000.

Dark column made up of water vapour

Dish for Doppler radar tracking

▲ WATERSPOUT
A waterspout is simply another name for a tornado over water. Though it looks like a solid column of water, it is mostly water vapour, which condenses out of rising warm air. Waterspouts are common over tropical and subtropical seas, where there is a ready supply of warm, moist air. They have the peculiar habit of picking up fish and frogs and dropping them over land.

tornadoes

▲ TRUCK-MOUNTED DOPPLER RADAR DISH
Radar helps experts give tornado warnings, and a form of radar known as Doppler has been in use since 1973. This detects mesocyclones, and can also track the direction of moving masses of rain and hail in big thunderclouds. In the United States, a network of fixed Doppler radar sites across the country keeps constant watch. This truck-mounted Doppler radar is used by "stormchasers", who follow tornadoes to study them at close quarters.

THE FUJITA SCALE ►
The Fujita Scale grades tornadoes by the damage they cause. Sixty-six per cent of the tornadoes reported annually in the United States are listed F0 and F1. The 2% that make up F4 and F5 account for more than two-thirds of fatalities.

THE FUJITA SCALE

F0	F1	F2	F3	F4	F5
Light damage: less than 118 kph (73 mph); some broken branches and chimneys	Moderate damage: 118–180 kph (73–112 mph); roofs peeled back, cars blown about	Considerable damage: 182–253 kph (113–157 mph); roofs torn off frame houses	Severe damage: 254–332 kph (158–206 mph); trains overturned, trees uprooted	Devastating damage: 333–419 kph (207–260 mph); well-built houses levelled	Incredible damage: 420–512 kph (261–318 mph); car-sized missiles fly through air

The eye of the storm, a calm area up to 50 km (31 miles) across

Whirling winds around the eye may reach speeds of up to 360 kph (224 mph)

HURRICANES

Hurricanes are the world's most destructive weather systems. They begin when thunderstorms mass together around a central area of low pressure. Also known as tropical cyclones, hurricanes form over tropical oceans, where warm waters create the necessary conditions. Once hurricanes have taken shape, they may travel thousands of kilometres, leaving a trail of devastation and breaking up only on reaching cold water or land. Scientists monitor hurricanes constantly in order to warn people living in high-risk zones, such as the Caribbean or the Bay of Bengal.

e▸▸
hurricanes

▲ PROGRESS OF HURRICANE
This sequence of images shows Hurricane Andrew approaching Florida (from right to left) on 24 August, 1992. The telltale spiral shape of a hurricane is created by cloud and rain bands sucked in towards the eye by spiralling winds. Meteorologists give personal names to hurricanes to encourage the public to listen to warning messages. At first, tropical cyclones were named after unpopular Australian politicians; today, men, women, animals, and trees all lend their names to storms.

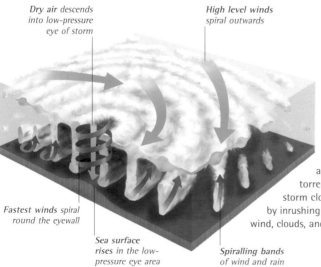

Dry air descends into low-pressure eye of storm

High level winds spiral outwards

Fastest winds spiral round the eyewall

Sea surface rises in the low-pressure eye area

Spiralling bands of wind and rain

◀ HURRICANE CROSS-SECTION
The heart of a hurricane is the eye, a column of calm air. Around it is the eyewall: a funnel of storm winds rotating at speeds of 120 kph (75 mph) or more. The eyewall carries warm, moist air upwards. This updraught creates low pressure at ground level, drawing in more warm air. The rising air cools and sheds torrential rain, then is hurled out over the storm clouds. Farther out, thunderstorms are fed by inrushing warm air to form towering walls of wind, clouds, and rain.

▶ BEAUFORT SCALE
The Beaufort Scale was devised in 1805 as a way of measuring wind speed at sea. Its 13 divisions range from calm conditions to hurricane force. In 1955, they were extended to 18 by the Saffir-Simpson Hurricane Scale, used to describe extremely violent storms.

① **Light air:** Average wind speed 3 kph (2 mph). Chimney smoke drifts gently.

② **Light breeze:** Wind speed 9 kph (5 mph). Leaves rustle. Wind felt on your face.

③ **Gentle breeze:** Wind speed 15 kph (10 mph). Leaves and twigs on trees move. Flags flutter.

④ **Moderate wind:** Wind speed 25 kph (15 mph). Small branches move. Paper blows around.

⑤ **Fresh wind:** Wind 35 kph (22 mph). S trees start to sway.

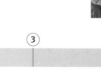

*Spiral bands of
cloud surround
the eye*

GLOBAL HURRICANE ACTIVITY

As their name indicates, tropical cyclones form only in tropical oceans. They are never less than five degrees north or south of the equator, on account of the Coriolis effect. This is when wind and ocean currents approaching the equator are pushed aside by Earth's rotational force. The Coriolis effect puts the first spin on a developing cyclone. To create the tremendous energy required to fuel a cyclone, the water temperature must be warm – at least 26.5°C (80°F) to a depth of 50 m (164 ft) or more. The heat and moisture not only start the cyclone, but also feed it. This explains why cyclones run out of energy when they cross cold ocean waters.

AFTERMATH OF ANDREW

...oats lie heaped like toys after Hurricane ...ndrew's passage over Florida in 1992. ...ndrew was a relatively small hurricane: ...urricane Gilbert (1988) was five times the ...ze. However, Andrew's winds were ...articularly violent, with gusts of up to ...62 kph (163 mph). The hurricane destroyed ...ore than 80,000 homes and caused ...S$26.5 billion worth of damage before it ran ...to the coast of Louisiana and broke up.

HURRICANE HUNTERS

In the United States, pilots of the 53rd Weather Reconnaissance Squadron search for tropical cyclones forming in the Atlantic, Caribbean Sea, Gulf of Mexico, and the eastern Pacific. They fly specially modified aircraft, carrying monitoring equipment, right into the eye of the storm. Telltale signs are storm clouds massing together around low-pressure areas. Sensors on parachutes are dropped into the storm to record temperature, wind speed, air pressure, and humidity. The readings are sent to the National Hurricane Center in Miami for analysis, and then distributed to meteorological centres around the world.

TREES UPROOTED BY STORM, KENT, UK ►
The "Great Storm" that struck southern England on 15–16 October, 1987, was the worst recorded since 1703. The 100-kph (62-mph) winds were well below hurricane force, but uprooted more than 15 million trees. They were in part caused by a true hurricane. Hurricane Floyd had hit the Caribbean a few days earlier and sent jet-stream winds thousands of kilometres east across the Atlantic towards Britain. These cold winds ran into warm, moist winds from the south, causing the storm.

 7   **8**   **9**   **10**   **11**   **12**

| ...wind: Wind (28 mph). Hard ...trol umbrella. ...ranches move. | Near gale: Wind speed 56 kph (35 mph). Whole trees sway. | Gale: Wind speed 68 kph (42 mph). Difficult to walk. Twigs broken off trees. | Severe gale: Wind speed 81 kph (50 mph). Slates and chimney pots blown off. | Storm: Wind speed 94 kph (58 mph). Houses damaged. Trees blown down. | Severe storm: Wind speed 110 kph (68 mph). Serious damage. | Hurricane: Wind speed more than 118 kph (73 mph). Widespread damage. |

TIMELINE OF EARTH DISCOVERIES

c.585BC According to the writers of his day, Thales of Miletus (in modern-day Turkey) correctly predicts a solar eclipse.

c.450BC Greek statesman Empedocles puts forward theory that everything is made entirely of four elements – earth, air, fire, and water – mixed in different proportions.

c.280BC Greek astronomer Aristarchus is the first to estimate the distance between Earth and the Sun. He is also the first to suggest that the planet rotates on its axis and revolves around the Sun, though few people believe him.

c.240BC Eratosthenes of Cyrene studies the angles of sunlight falling on two towns in Egypt, and from them he measures the circumference of Earth as 41,143 km (25,700 miles). He is accurate to within 1,000 km (800 miles).

AD23 Greek geographer and historian Strabo publishes his *Geographical Sketches*. In them he notes that earthquakes and volcanoes cause lands to rise and sink; he proposes cold, temperate, and tropical climate zones; and he suggests Earth is so big there might be continents still to discover.

AD79 Roman Pliny the Younger writes the first account of a volcanic eruption, describing Mount Vesuvius.

c.130 Chinese scientist Chang Heng designs the first seismograph. His "earthquake weathercock" uses finely balanced metal balls that fall when the ground shakes.

c.140 Greek astronomer and mathematician Ptolemy claims the Earth is at the centre of the Universe, and that the Sun and planets revolve around it.

c.975 Muslim scholars in Basra (Iraq) publish *The Aim of the Sage*, an encyclopedia that describes rock layers.

1086 Chinese astronomer and engineer Shen Kua describes rock erosion, sedimentation, and uplift and explains the origins of fossils.

c.1100 Chinese invent the magnetic compass. It uses a pivoting magnetized needle to point to Earth's poles.

1492 Genoese merchant Christopher Columbus is sponsored by Spain to find a western route to China. But his maps (based on Ancient Greek and Biblical geography) are wrong. He lands in the Caribbean instead (believing it to be Japan), and is credited with discovering America.

c.1500 Italian artist and scientist Leonardo da Vinci suggests that fossil shells in hillside rocks are remains of animals that once lived in the sea.

1519–21 Portuguese navigator Ferdinand Magellan sets out to be the first to sail around the world. He is killed in the Philippines, but his surviving sailors complete the circumnavigation.

c.1540 German scientist Georgius Agricola publishes a scientific classification of minerals (then known as fossils).

1543 Polish astronomer Nicolaus Copernicus publishes his theory that Earth rotates on its axis daily and revolves annually around the Sun.

1600 English scientist William Gilbert publishes his experiments which showed that Earth is a giant magnet, whose north and south poles roughly coincide with its geographic poles.

1609 Italian astronomer Galileo Galilei uses a telescope to offer the first scientific proof for Copernicus's theory. Using his telescope, Galileo found that Venus went through phases, just like our Moon, and that these phases could only be explained by Venus going around the Sun and not Earth.

1620 English thinker Francis Bacon notices that the coasts of Africa and South America fit like pieces of a jigsaw.

1644 Italian physicist Evangelista Torricelli invents the mercury barometer, an instrument that measures atmospheric pressure.

1650 English Archbishop James Ussher adds up the ages of characters in the Bible to calculate the birth of the Universe in 4004 BC. His view is widely accepted until the 19th century.

1655 Ferdinand II, grand duke of Tuscany and a pupil of Galileo, invents the condensation hygrometer (which measures humidity) and the thermometer (which measures temperature).

1669 Danish geologist Nicolaus Steno describes crystal formation in quartz. He recognizes that some rocks are formed from sediment, and that the history of Earth can be studied by looking at rock layers.

1679 English astronomer Edmund Halley recognizes that the Sun's warmth creates atmospheric movement, and links air pressure with altitude. He predicts the return of Halley's comet in 1705.

1687 English scientist Isaac Newton publishes *Mathematical Principles of Natural Philosophy* (known as the *Principia*) which sets out to explain the basic laws whi govern motion, gravity, and the Universe.

1735 English physicist George Hadle explains how Earth's rotation affects trade winds. His name is given to Ha cells, which are an element of global air circulation patterns.

1795 Scottish geologist James Hutt challenges the popular Bible-based belief that Earth is only 6000 years old He claims that the processes now shaping Earth's crust (such as sedimentation and erosion) have been doing so for much longer.

1804 French zoologist Georges Cuvie studies ancient fossils and suggests they are "thousands of centuries" ol He believes that long-extinct animals were kille off by natural catastrophes, such as floods.

1806 English Admiral Francis Beaufor devises a scale of wind speed fo sailors at sea. It was later modified for land us by substituting features such as cars and trees

1815 English engineer William Smith publishes the first geologic map He shows that, depending on where they are found in rock layers, fossils prove whether one layer is older than another.

1822 English amateur palaeontologist Mary Anne Mantell discovers the first fossils (large teeth) of a giant creature, later identified as a dinosaur by English scientist Richard Owen.

1827 French mathematician Jean Baptiste Fourier introduces the greenhouse effect. He says Earth has the "effect of glass" in trapping heat from the Sun.

1830 Scotsman Sir Charles Lyell publishes his first edition of *Principles of Geology*. He suggests that Earth is hundreds of millions of years old.

1831 English explorer James Clark Ross finds the magnetic north pole.

1837 US geologist James Dana suggests that landscapes are shaped by continuing forces of weathering and erosion, rather than by sudden catastrophic events such as earthquakes and volcanoes.

1840 Swiss-born scientist Louis Agassiz puts forward his theory of ice ages, and proposes that northern Europe was once covered in an ice sheet.

872–76 HMS *Challenger*, under the direction of British Admiralty and the Royal Society, [make]s the first thorough scientific exploration [of th]e sea-bed. It travels 127,600 km ([79]90 miles) on a four-year voyage mapping [the w]orld's oceans.

874–75 Charles Sigsbee of the US Navy pioneers new [met]hods of ocean-floor mapping (bathymetry) [in] his survey of the Gulf of Mexico on board [the] steamer *Blake*.

880 English geologist John Milne invents the modern seismograph [ins]trument for measuring earthquakes).

895 Swedish chemist Svante Arrhenius suggests that carbon [dio]xide added to Earth's atmosphere helps trap [hea]t from the Sun, leading to global warming.

903 Norwegian explorer Roald Amundsen makes the first [voy]age through the Northwest Passage (a sea [cor]ridor through the Arctic ice that connects [the] Atlantic and Pacific Oceans).

903 Norwegian scientist Kristian Birkeland explains how the [nor]thern lights are created.

904 New Zealand scientist Ernest Rutherford explains [ra]dioactive decay. This discovery will lead to [ra]diometric dating, a method used to calculate [th]e age of rocks.

906 Irish-born geologist Richard Oldham finds evidence [fo]r Earth's iron core after studying seismic [w]aves produced by earthquakes.

909 Austrian geologist Eduard Suess writes *The Face of the Earth*, [w]hich explains how Earth's processes [s]hape the mountains and oceans. It also [m]akes first mention of the ancient [s]upercontinent Gondwanaland.

1910 Croatian scientist Andrija Mohorovicic studies seismic [w]aves and discovers the boundary between [E]arth's crust and mantle. This is known as the [M]ohorovicic discontinuity, or simply the Moho.

1911–12 Roald Amundsen leads the first successful [ex]pedition to reach the South Pole, beating [E]nglishman Captain Scott.

1912 German meteorologist Alfred Wegener publishes his [c]ontinental drift theory, claiming that all the [c]ontinents were once joined together in a [s]upercontinent he called Pangaea. However, [m]ost scientists ignore it until the 1960s.

1920 Serbian scientist Milutin Milankovitch discovers the link between climate and solar radiation. He bases it on variations in Earth's orbit around the Sun – the "Milankovitch wobble".

1921 Norwegian meteorologist Vilhelm Bjerknes publishes the major study on the atmosphere. Bjerknes, who identifies air masses and fronts, is the father of modern weather forecasting.

1922 British physicist Lewis Richardson uses mathematical calculations to forecast the weather – a method that becomes practical much later, when computers are invented.

1924 US astronomer Edwin Hubble shows that nebulae (clouds where stars are formed) exist far beyond the Milky Way. In 1929 he shows that the Universe is expanding.

1927 Belgian astronomer Georges Lemaître proposes Big Bang theory of the origins of the Universe.

1931 English geologist Arthur Holmes publishes his geologic timescale. Based on radioactivity, he estimated Earth to be 4 billion years old. Importantly, he proposed a theory of continental drift to explain Wegener's theory, suggesting convection currents in the mantle.were responsible for moving the tectonic plates.

1934 US naturalist Charles Beebe and engineer Otis Barton make a world record descent of 923 m (3,028 ft) in the bathysphere, pioneering deep-sea exploration.

1935 US physicist Charles Richter invents the Richter Scale for reporting the strength of earthquakes.

1935 US geophysicist Maurice Ewing takes the first seismic readings in the open sea. He links earthquakes to seafloor spreading from mid-ocean ridges.

1936 Danish seismologist Inge Lehmann claims that Earth's core has a solid inner and a liquid outer part. (Nuclear tests later prove her correct.)

1948–77 US mapmakers Marie Tharp and Bruce Heezen begin using sonar readings to map the ridges and other features of ocean floors. They publish the World Ocean Floor map in 1977. Their discoveries help scientists accept the tectonic plates theory in the 1960s.

1953 US scientist Clair Patterson calculates the age of Earth. At 4.5 billion years, it is the first close estimate in the history of geology.

1959 US scientists on board the Coast and Geodetic Survey Ship *Pioneer* discover the Mid-Atlantic Ridge Rift Valley. This is the most significant bathymetric discovery made up to that time.

1959–62 US geologist Harry Hess's theory of seafloor spreading contributes to the acceptance of plate tectonics theory. He uses echo sounding to collect ocean floor profiles.

1963 British scientists Frederick Vine and Drummond Matthews realize that magnetic stripes in sea-bed crust along mid-ocean ridges show that Earth's north-south magnetic polarity reverses regularly. Provides support for Hess's model of seafloor spreading.

1963 Canadian geologist John Tuzo Wilson introduces the theory of hot spots: rising plumes of magma in Earth's mantle that heat the crust. He uses it to explain how islands such as the Hawaiian chain are created.

1964 *Alvin* makes its maiden voyage of exploration. This submersible, run by the Woods Hole Oceanographic Institution in the USA, pioneers research and exploration in deep oceans. It provides the first observation of deep-sea hydrothermal activity.

1965 John Tuzo Wilson proposes a third type of plate boundary that connects the oceanic ridges and trenches: the transform-fault boundary. The best-known example of this is the San Andreas Fault zone.

1969 On 20 July, the lunar module from the NASA Apollo 11 space mission puts the first man on the Moon.

1979 English scientist James Lovelock suggests that Earth's systems work together as a giant, living organism. This idea is called the Gaia hypothesis.

1980 US scientists Luis and Walter Alvarez claim that a meteorite that struck near Mexico 65 million years ago could have created the climate change that killed off the dinosaurs.

1985 Scientists of the British Antarctic Survey record a springtime hole in Earth's ozone layer over Antarctica.

1996 Scientists claim that a meteorite found in Antarctica has come from Mars. It contains structures which may prove that water – and life – once existed on the distant planet.

2004 NASA lands two robot vehicles, *Spirit* and *Opportunity*, on Mars to explore the planet's geology and to search for evidence of water and life.

GLOSSARY

Abyssal Relating to the deep ocean floor beyond the continental margin.

Air mass A large body of air with a uniform temperature.

Anticyclone A weather system in which winds circulate around a high pressure area.

Archipelago A group of islands forming a cluster or chain.

Asteroid A body of rock, smaller than a planet, that orbits the Sun. Most asteroids in the Solar System are found in the asteroid belt, between the orbits of Jupiter and Mars.

Asthenosphere The weak layer of mantle immediately below the rigid lithosphere.

Atoll See *Coral reef*.

Atmosphere A layer of gas held around a planet or moon by its gravity.

Aurora The flickering lights produced over polar regions when solar wind particles hit the upper atmosphere. These lights are known as aurora borealis in the north, and aurora australis in the south.

Basalt Earth's most common volcanic rock, making up most of the crust under the oceans.

Biome The broadest classification of a community of plants and animals.

Biosphere All living organisms of the Earth and its atmosphere.

Black smoker see *Hydrothermal system*.

Caldera A collapsed crater at the summit of a volcano.

Comet A body of dust and ice that orbits the Sun.

Carbon The chemical element found in all living things, and many rocks and minerals. The carbon cycle is the transfer of carbon to and from the atmosphere.

Cirque A steep-sided, rounded hollow carved out at the head of a glacier.

Comet A body of dust and ice that orbits the Sun.

Condensation The transformation of a substance from a gas to a liquid.

Coniferous Cone-bearing evergreen trees, such as pines and firs, which usually have needle-like leaves. Coniferous trees make up the belt of forest around the lands of the far north, known as the boreal (or taiga in Eurasia).

Continent A very large landmass, for example Eurasia, Antarctica, or North America.

Continental margin The part of a continent along a coast and including the continental shelf and continental slope.

Continental shelf A shallow marine zone between dry land and the deep sea.

Continental slope A steep gradient between the continental margin and the deep sea-bed.

Convection The movement and circulation of gases and liquids in response to temperature changes.

Coral A plant-like animal made up of many small individuals – polyps – living together and sharing resources, such as food.

Coral reef A structure built up in shallow tropical seas by the activity of corals and other organisms. A reef that has grown on top of a sunken extinct volcano is called an atoll.

Core The intensely hot innermost layer of Earth, made up of a solid inner core and liquid outer core, both made of nickel and iron.

Crater The bowl-shaped opening at the summit of a volcano, through which an erupting volcano discharges gases and lava. Also a circular depression in a landscape caused by a meteorite impact.

Crust The outermost layer of solid Earth, consisting of continental and oceanic crust.

Crystal A solid, such as a mineral in a rock, whose atoms are arranged in an orderly pattern.

Current A flow of water or air.

Cyclone An area of low atmospheric pressure in which warm winds rise in a spiral. A tropical cyclone is another name for a hurricane.

Deciduous Relating to a tree that sheds its leaves in the autumn.

Deep-sea trench A canyon-like depression in the ocean floor where one tectonic plate has slid beneath another.

Delta An area of sediment deposition built up by some rivers where they enter a sea or lake.

Deposition The laying down of material such as sand and gravel in new locations, usually by wind, water, or ice.

Desert A region where water is lost more rapidly than it is gained through precipitation.

Dune A mound of loose sand shaped by the wind.

Earthquake A sudden motion or trembling in the Earth caused by release along a fault.

Ecosystem A community of life-forms and their local environment.

El Niño A combined ocean and atmospheric event, taking place every 2–7 years, in which warm water currents in the Pacific Ocean flow east instead of west.

Equator An imaginary line around the middle Earth that is at equal distance from the poles.

Erosion The general process that loosens, dissolves, or wears away the materials of Earth crust and moves them from one place to another.

Eruption An outpouring of magma from within Earth. Magma that flows on Earth's surface is known as lava.

Fault A fracture in rock along which rock masses move – the source of earthquakes.

Fog Condensed droplets of water forming in the air at ground level.

Fossil The remains, imprint, or trace of a life-form preserved in rock.

Front The forward-moving edge of an air mass. An occluded front is a boundary in the atmosphere where cold air catches up with warm air and raises it off the ground.

Geothermal energy Electric power that is generated from steam produced by hot rocks, usually associated with volcanic activity.

Glaciation The formation and movement of glaciers or ice sheets.

Glacier A mass of of ice on land that flows slowly under gravity's influence. Valley glaciers flow down existing valleys. Piedmont glaciers form where several valley glaciers join at the base of a mountain range. An ice sheet is a vast layer of ice, that can cover large areas. Icecaps are smaller domes of ice covering a mountain.

Global warming The rise in temperature of Earth's atmosphere.

Greenhouse effect Trapping of the Sun's heat in the atmosphere by gases and particles.

Groundwater Precipitation that soaks into and is stored in the ground, rather than running off into rivers or evaporating.

Gyre A circular water current in an ocean.

Habitat The natural and usual living space of a plant or animal.

Hot spot A site of volcanic activity in Earth's crust created by rising magma from the mantle.

Humus Nutrient-rich matter, found in the upper layers of soil, that is produced from dead or decaying plants and animals.

Hurricane A destructive storm whipped up by energy released from rising warm winds.

...othermal system Hot ground water that ...lates in Earth's crust. Igneous rocks are the ... source of heat. When the heated water, ...hed with dissolved minerals, escapes from ...eafloor it produces discoloured springs, ...wn as "black smokers". The land equivalent ...own as a hot spring.

...ge A cold period in Earth's history.

...erg A floating block of ice that has broken ... a coastal glacier or ice sheet.

...ap see *Glacier*.

...sheet see *Glacier*.

...eous rock Rock formed when lava or magma ...s and crystallizes.

...nd arc A chain of volcanic islands created ...r sites of volcanic activity.

...bar A contour line on a weather map that ...ws variations in atmospheric pressure.

... stream Fast, cold wind current blowing at ...h altitude.

...goon A calm body of water enclosed by ...dbanks or the reefs of a coral atoll.

...nar A fast-flowing stream of loose ash, rock, ...d mud that runs off a volcano's side, ...mmonly set off by heavy rainfall.

...ndslide see *Mass movement*.

...va Magma that erupts and flows on Earth's ...rface. It cools after eruption to form rock.

...ghtning Discharge of electricity within a ...undercloud or from a thundercloud to the ...ound. A stroke of lightning can heat the air ... temperatures of up to 30,000°C (54,000°F).

...thosphere The rigid, outermost part of Earth's ...yers – includes the crust and uppermost part ...f the mantle.

...agma Molten rock below Earth's surface.

...lagnetosphere The magnetic forcefield in and ...round Earth, created by movement of iron in ...he planet's core. It protects Earth from the ...harged particles that stream out from the Sun.

...Mantle The middle layer of Earth's three main ...ayers, up to 2,870km (1,800 miles) thick.

...lass movement A movement of rock or soil ...o lower ground as a result of gravity. ...ncludes landslides.

Mesosphere The layer of the atmosphere above ...the stratosphere.

Metamorphic rock Rock changed from its ...original state by heat and pressure.

Meteor A bright streak of light formed when a lump of space rock heats up on entering Earth's atmosphere. Any space rock that strikes Earth is called a meteorite.

Mid-ocean ridge An underwater volcanic mountain range that forms along a diverging tectonic plate boundary.

Mineral A naturally occurring, inorganic solid with a regular internal composition. Earth's rocks are made up of minerals.

Oasis A place in a desert where the presence of groundwater near the surface allows vegetation to grow.

Occluded front see *Front*.

Ore A natural material from which valuable minerals can be profitably extracted.

Ozone A form of oxygen. It can occur at ground level, but is found mostly in a layer in the stratosphere, where it filters some of the Sun's harmful ultraviolet light.

Photosynthesis The process in which organisms use sunlight to convert carbon dioxide and water into oxygen and sugars.

Planet A large, spherical mass in space that orbits a sun.

Plate boundary The location in Earth's crust where tectonic plates are in contact. There are three kinds of plate boundaries: convergent (where plates move together), divergent (where they move apart), and transform (where one is sliding past the other).

Precipitation Water that falls to ground in the form of rain, hail, or snow.

Pressure system The variations in atmospheric pressure that affect the local weather. While high pressure usually produces clear, dry skies, low pressure can lead to rain, hail, or thunder.

Pyroclastic Relating to material such as ash (volcanic glass and rock) ejected by a volcanic eruption. A pyroclastic flow is a deadly avalanche of hot ash, rock, and gases.

Rainforest Forest with lush growth produced by high rainfall – above 2,500mm (98 in) a year.

Rift valley A depression in Earth's crust formed when landmasses are moving apart.

Rock A hard substance made up of one or more minerals. Some volcanic rocks are glassy.

Sediment The particles of rock, mineral, or organic matter that are transported in streams before settling on marine, river, or lake beds.

Sedimentary rock Rock formed from sediment that has been buried and squeezed by pressure from above.

Seismic wave A shockwave produced by an earthquake.

Soil Loose surface material produced by the weathering of rock or sediment and the addition of humus.

Stalactite A cone-shaped structure created when groundwater deposits minerals on a cave roof. A stalagmite is a pedestal-shaped structure created when water drips from the tip of a stalactite and deposits minerals on a cave floor.

Star A massive ball of burning gases in space that produces heat and light from the nuclear reaction in its core. The Sun is our local star.

Stratosphere The layer of Earth's atmosphere above the troposphere.

Subduction The sinking of an oceanic plate beneath a neighbouring plate at a tectonic plate boundary.

Tectonic plate Any one of about 17 pieces of Earth's rigid shell (made up of the crust and uppermost part of the upper mantle) that drifts slowly over the planet's surface in a process known as plate tectonics.

Temperate A region at high latitudes affected by seasonal change.

Thermosphere The outermost layer of Earth's atmosphere.

Tide The regular rise and fall of seawater on a coast, mostly governed by the pull of the Moon's gravity on the oceans.

Tornado A destructive whirling wind that forms between a cloud and the ground surface.

Troposphere The layer of the atmosphere that is closest to Earth's surface.

Tsunami An ocean wave triggered by an earthquake, submarine landslide, or volcano.

Typhoon see *Hurricane*.

Volcano The site of an eruption of molten rock from within Earth. The build-up of erupted lava usually produces a cone. A stratovolcano explosively ejects both lava and pyroclastic material and has steep sides. A shield volcano is produced when highly fluid lava flows spread out to form a broad, gently sloping mountain.

Wave A form of energy transfer through water, air, or earth.

Wavelength The distance between the crest (highest point) and trough (lowest point) of a wave.

Weathering The process by which rock is disintegrated and decomposed by wind, water, frost, and organisms on Earth's surface.

INDEX

A page number in **bold** refers to the main entry for that subject.

ACKNOWLEDGEMENTS

Dorling Kindersley would like to thank Lynn Bresler for proof-reading and the index; Margaret Parrish for Americanization; and Rosie O'Neill for editorial support.

Dorling Kindersley Ltd is not responsible and does not accept liability for the availability or content of any web site other than its own, or for any exposure to offensive, harmful, or inaccurate material that may appear on the Internet. Dorling Kindersley Ltd will have no liability for any damage or loss caused by viruses that may be downloaded as a result of looking at and browsing the web sites that it recommends. Dorling Kindersley downloadable images are the sole copyright of Dorling Kindersley Ltd, and may not be reproduced, stored, or transmitted in any form or by any means for any commercial or profit-related purpose without prior written permission of the copyright owner.

Picture Credits

The publisher would like to thank the following for their kind permission to reproduce their photographs:

Abbreviations key:
t-top, b-bottom, r-right, l-left, c-centre, a-above, f-far

0: Getty Images/Antony Edwards/James Balog; 1: NASA (c); 2: Alamy Images/Glen Allison (c); 3: Zefa Visual Media (c); 4: Alamy Images/Tom Pfeiffer; 6: NASA (cr); 7: NASA (cl); 8: Corbis/Bryan Allen (b), Science Photo Library/Detlev van Ravenswaay (tr), Science Photo Library/National Optical Astronomy Observatories (cr), Science Photo Library/National Optical Astronomy Observatories (cfr), Science Photo Library/Space Telescope Science Institute (c); 9: NASA (b), Science Photo Library/European Southern Observatory (tr), Science Photo Library/Francois Gohier (br); 10: Corbis/David Bartruff (b), DK Images/NASA (cfl), NASA (bl); 11: DK Images/NASA/Finley Holiday Films (b), Science Photo Library/John Heseltine (tr), Science Photo Library/John Heseltine (cra), Science Photo Library/John Heseltine (cr), Science Photo Library/John Heseltine (cfr), Science Photo Library/Victor Habbick Visions (ca); 12: Corbis/Kennan Ward (l), Image courtesy Earth Science World ImageBank/NASA/JPL (t), Image courtesy Earth Science World ImageBank/NOAA (br), Science Photo Library/Space Telescope Science Institute/NASA (tr); 13: Corbis/Brian A. Vikander (br), DK Images/Courtesy of The British Library (tr), DK Images/Stephen Oliver (l); 14: Corbis/George D Lepp (cr), Getty Images/Helena Vallis (bl); 15: Corbis/Bryan Allen (c), Corbis/Hubert Stadler (br), Science Photo Library/Alexis Rosenfeld (r), Science Photo Library/John Eastcott & Yva Momatiuk (cr), Getty Images/Nicolas Parfitt (crb); 16: Corbis/Jim Sugar (l), Corbis/Lester V Bergman (cl), Science Photo Library/Georgette Douwma (br); 17: Corbis/James L Amos (cl); Corbis/M L Sinibaldi (bl), Corbis/Peter Johnson (br), DK Images/Dave King/Courtesy of the National Museum of Wales (tr), DK Images/Harry Taylor /Natural History Museum (cr), Science Photo Library/D. van Ravenswaay (tl); 19: Corbis/Richard Cummins (car), GeoScience Features Picture Library/Dr B Booth (cal), Getty Images/Greg Pease (cla); 20: Corbis/Jason Burke/Eye Ubiquitous (tl); 21: Corbis (tl), Corbis (cl); Corbis/Original image courtesy of NASA (cfl), Corbis/Kevin Schafer (bl), DK Images/Harry Taylor/Courtesy of the Royal Museum of Scotland, Edinburgh (cb), DK Images/Harry Taylor/Courtesy of the University Museum of Zoology, Cambridge (br); 23: Corbis/Bouhet Richard (br), Corbis/Roger Ressmeyer (tr), US Geological Survey/USGS (cr); 24: Science Photo Library/Bernard Edmaier (tr); USGS (cl); 25: Corbis/Hans Strand (br); Corbis/Ralph White (cl), DK Images/Gables (tr), Science Photo Library/G Brad Lewis (clb), US Geological Survey/J B Judd (tl), US Geological Survey/R. L. Christiansen (bl); 26: Corbis/Jonathan Blair (bl), Corbis/Yann Arthus-Bertrand (c), DK Images/James Stevenson/Courtesy of the Museo Archeologico Nazionale di Napoli (c); 27: Corbis/Yann Arthus-Bertrand (br), Powerstock/Phillippe Bourseiller (cr), Science Photo Library/Robert M Carey, Science Photo Library/NOAA (tr), US Geological Survey/USGS (cl); 28: Corbis/Lloyd Cluff (cfr), Image courtesy Earth Science World ImageBank (bl), Image courtesy Earth Science World ImageBank/Chris Keane/American Geological Institute (br), Panos Pictures (cl); 29: Corbis (tl), Corbis/Bettmann (br), US Geological Survey (bl), US Geological Survey/C. E. Meyer (cl); 30: DK Images/John Lepine/Science Museum, London (bl), Panos Pictures/Jim Holmes (tr); 31: Corbis/Reuters (t), Science Photo Library/Carlos Munoz-Yague/Eurelios (cl), Science Photo Library/NASA (cr); 32: Corbis/Lloyd Cluff; 33: Corbis (t), Corbis/Bettmann (cl), Corbis/George Hall (c), Corbis/Roger Rossmeyer (br); 34: Alamy Images/Colin Monteath/Worldwid Picture Library (l); 35: Alamy Images/Chris Howes/Wild Places Photography (cfr), Corbis/Pablo Corral Vega (br), DK Images/Colin Keates/Courtesy of the Natural History Museum, London (tr), Image courtesy Earth Science World ImageBank/Bruce Molnia, Terra Photographics (clb), Image courtesy Earth Science World ImageBank/Martin Miller/University of Oregon (tl), Image courtesy Earth Science World ImageBank/National Park Service (cb); 36: Corbis/Lloyd Cluff (c), Science Photo Library/Gary Hincks (bl), US Geological Survey/R. L. Schuster (r); 37: Corbis/Kike Arnal (cr), Lowell Georgia (br), US Geological Survey/Tom Lynch (tc), US Geological Survey/Tom Lynch (tr); 38: DK Images/Andreas Einsiedel (br), DK Images/Colin Keates (br), DK Images/Colin Keates (br), Image courtesy Earth Science World ImageBank (bl), Image courtesy Earth Science World ImageBank/Martin Miller/University of Oregon (cl), Tony Waltham Geophotos (cl), Tony Waltham Geophotos (l); 39: Tony Waltham Geophotos (c); 40: Image courtesy Earth Science World ImageBank/ASARCO (cbl), Science Photo Library/Dirk Wiersma (r); 41: Image courtesy Earth Science World ImageBank/Dr. Richard Busch (tr), Image courtesy Earth Science World ImageBank/Stonetrust Inc (bc), GeoScience Features Picture Library/Dr B Booth (c), Science Photo Library/Simon Fraser (br); 42: Corbis/Joseph Sohm/ChromoSohm Inc (t),

Corbis/William Manning (bc); 43: Corbis/Brian A Vikander (tr), Corbis/John M Roberts (cr), Corbis/Tiziana & Gianni Baldizzone (br); 44: Corbis/Nik Wheeler (b), Getty Images/Stone/Paul Chesley (bl), Science Photo Library/M-Sat Ltd (car), Science Photo Library/Worldsat International (cfl), Still Pictures/Qinetiq (tcr); 45: Corbis/Galen Rowell (tl), GeoScience Features Picture Library/Dr B Booth (c), Still Pictures/Gunter Ziesler (r), Still Pictures/Truchet/UNEP (bc); 46: Bryan And Cherry Alexander Photography/J Hyde (l); 47: Bryan And Cherry Alexander Photography (tr), Corbis (tl), Corbis/Chris Rainier (bl), Corbis Ralph/A Clevenger (br), Science Photo Library/British Antarctic Survey (bc), Science Photo Library/Tony Craddock (cl); 48: Corbis/Richard Hamilton Smith (r); 49: Corbis/Julia Waterlow/Eye Ubiquitous (tr); DK Images/Alan Watson (r), Image courtesy Earth Science World ImageBank/NASA Visible Earth (br), National Resources Conservation (tc), National Resources Conservation (c), National Resources Conservation (cb), Science Photo Library/David Nanuk (bl); 50: Corbis/Dean Conger (t), Corbis/Layne Kennedy (br), Corbis/Nik Wheeler (br), Corbis/Wolfgang Kaehler (bl); 51: Corbis (tl), Corbis/Christine Osborne (cl), Corbis/Richard Hamilton Smith (cl), Corbis/Roger Wood (tr), Corbis/Roger Wood (cl), Panos Pictures (cr), Panos Pictures (br); 52: Corbis/David Muench (r), Corbis/Robert Gill/Papilo (c), Zefa Visual Media/G Rossenbach (bl); 53: Corbis/Reuters (br), Zefa Visual Media/G. Rossenbach (bl); 54: Corbis/Michelle Westmorland (l); 55: Nature Picture Library/Rhonda Klevansky (r), Corbis (t), Getty Images/Stone/Mark Wagner (c); 56: Corbis/Jeremy Horner (bl), Science Photo Library/Gregory Ochocki (br); 57: Corbis/Kevin Schafer (br), Corbis/Michael & Patricia Fogden (cr); 58: Still Pictures/P. Labarbe (l); 59: Corbis/John M Roberts (tl), Woodfall Wild Images (bl), Woodfall Wild Images (r); 60: DK Images/Gables (br), DK Images/Jerry Young (br), Getty Images/Nicholas Parfitt (c); 61: Corbis/Bettmann (br), Corbis/W. Wayne Lockwood, M.D. (t), DK Images/Peter Anderson (cfr); 62: Science Photo Library/Martin Dohrn (clb); 63: Alamy Images/Robert Harding World Imagery (clb), Oxford Scientific Films/Daniel Cox (crb), Still Pictures/F.Ardito/UNEP (tr), Getty Images/Randy Wells (r); 64: Corbis/Graham Neden/Ecoscene (cbr); 64-65: Corbis/Hans Strand (r), Getty Images/Peter Scoones (b); 65: DK Images/Neil Fletcher (crb); 66: Corbis/Robert Yin (cl), Corbis/Stephen Frink (clb); 66-67:Getty Images/Mike Kelly (c); 67: Science Photo Library/Andrew Syred (tcr), Science Photo Library/B. Murton/Southampton Oceanography Centre (cr), Science Photo Library/British Antarctic Survey (tc), Science Photo Library/Laguna Design (cr), Getty Images/Mike Kelly (tl), Getty Images/Peter David (cb); 68: Still Pictures/Peter Schickert (tr); 68-69: Corbis/Robert Y. Ono (b); 69: Corbis/Jim Sugar (tr), Corbis/Jonathan Blair (clb); Corbis/Natalie Fobes (cla); Corbis/Philip Gould (bl); Corbis/Tom Brakefield (cbr), Science Photo Library/NOAA (tl); 70: Science Photo Library/Martin Bond (cfl); 71: Associated Press (crb), Corbis/Lloyd Cluff (bl), NOAA (tc); 72: Corbis/Hubert Stadler (tr), Pa Photos/EPA

(bc); 73: Corbis/Richard T. Nowitz (bc),Corbis/Vince Streano (br), Seapics.com Mark Conlin (bl), NOAA (tr), Science Photo Library/R.B.Husar/NASA (tr); 74: Corbis/Ch McLaughlin (tr), Corbis/Layne Kennedy (c Science Photo Library/Colin Cuthbert (cfl) Science Photo Library/W.Haxby, Lamont-Doherty Earth Observatory (bc); 75: Natur Picture Library/Florian Graner (cb), Stephe Productions Inc (br); 76: European Space Agency (tr), Science Photo Library/Mike Bo /Agstock (clb), Zefa Visual Media (tl); 77: A Images/ImageState (bl), Science Photo Library/NASA (c), Getty Images/Arnulf Hus (cfr), Zefa Visual Media (tr); 78: Corbis/Jac Langevin (l), Powerstock/Peter Adama (bl), Science Photo Library/British Antarctic Sur (br); 78-79: Science Photo Library/NASA(t 79: Corbis/Gary Braasch (crb), Corbis/Lowe Georgia (tr); 80: Corbis (tl); 81: Corbis/Reut (clb), Corbis/Richard Cummins (clb), Corbis/Roger Ressmeyer (t), Getty Images/Angelo Cavalli (cfl); 82: Corbis/Reut (l), DK Images/Brian Cosgrove (c), DK Images/Brian Cosgrove (crb); 83: Corbis/Hu Stadler (clb); Corbis/Rob Matheson (r), Corbis/Tiziana and Gianni Baldizzone (cbl), Science Photo Library/Jim Reed (c), Science Photo Library/Ted Kinsman (ca); 84: NASA (Science Photo Library (br); Science Photo Library/NASA (tr); 85: Alamy Images/Michae Dwyer (bl), aviation-images.com/Mark Wagr (tr), Science Photo Library/British Antarctic Survey (cla), Science Photo Library/British Antarctic Survey (cfr), Science Photo Library/Hank Morgan (bc); 86: Oxford Scient Films/Warren Faidley (c), Oxford Scientific Films/Warren Faidley (r), Oxford Scientific Films/Warren Faidley (br), Oxford Scientific Films/Warren Faidley (cfr); 87: Corbis (tl), Corbis/Jim Reed (cfr), Corbis/Ray Soto (cfl), Hulton Archive/Getty Images (cra); 88-89: Corbis/Reuters (b); 89: Science Photo Library/Chris Sattlberger (cb), Getty Images/E Pritchard (br); 94: Corbis/Bill Varie (l); 95: Corbis/Bill Varie (r).

Jacket images
Front: Corbis: Steve Wilkings (cfr); Science Photo Library: Krafft/Explorer (tr), NASA (cl). **Spine:** Corbis: Steve Wilkings. **Back:** Corbis: (cl); Science Photo Library: Mehau Kulyk (cr).

All other images © Dorling Kindersley. For further information see: **www.dkimages.com**